JUST WIGGLE
YOUR TOES

Written By:

Kevin Brooks & Jeff DeAngelis

CONTENTS

◆ ◆ ◆

Through a series of interviews with the people who lived through this tragic event we hope this book is an awakening for young readers to learn the dangers of drinking and driving. How one man's unfortunate incident told by those closest to him and how it permanently altered their lives. By the end, we also choose to leave you with a message of hope for the future.

PROLOGUE

The car hit the curb with such force it sent it airborne. My 1991 Chevy Cavalier has taken flight. – Until... It came crashing down on the nose and toppled end over end. Just a pile of mutilated metal and debris strewn across a dark Canadian highway. I must've been going 130kmh or 80mph and I never saw the turn coming. I was intoxicated, no check that, I was hammered and should never have been behind the wheel. But that night I thought I could "make it" like I had so many times before. Now I lay here, upside down covered in blood and motor fluids. My friend is wedged in the seat beside me, I didn't know it yet, but he'll die from his injuries and I'll never walk again. I won't learn these painful truths until weeks from now when I awake from my medically induced coma. Unconscious and trapped, I can't move. Nothing but the red brake lights glowing in the night and the whir of the wheels still spinning. I'm fading out now. I can't feel anything anymore. I can't even wiggle my toes.

1

Kevin: The Crash, and What I Can Remember

"One second was music, joy and fun times with my buddy and the next... The lights turned out. Darkness. Nothing."

It was Friday June 23rd when I got off work from the cell phone store. And I drove the ten-minute drive home. It was a beautiful summer night. I was just figuring out my life. I had just turned 21 years old and only been driving about a year now. Good vibes were in the air, it was the beginning of summer and just starting to get warm. I was excited for the weekend ahead. When I got home, I found my dad and neighbors in the garage where they would always hang out. I stayed with them a short while just chatting about nothing at all. Simple conversations I think we sometimes take for granted. I went inside and up to my room to shower and change into a suit, which is a rarity for me. I grew up skateboarding, so typically the only thing I wore were Tee shirts and skate shoes. But on this night, I had to get dressed up for my sister, Allison's graduation. Allison was just a few years younger than me and was about to celebrate this big moment in her life at a posh private school near our home. This wasn't her high school nor mine, just an auditorium where the ceremony was held. In fact, I never really had a formal graduation. I would tend to choose skating, partying and mischief over class far more often than I should have in secondary school. So this was a particularly big night for our family. Allison was the first Brooks sibling to walk across a stage and accept a diploma. So, after putting on this ridiculous suit I went down to meet the rest of my family at the school.

Allison's graduation was a great start to the weekend. There were positive vibes all around and a urge to celebrate this monumental event. It was early Friday evening at this point, and I knew from my friends that there was a party going on somewhere tonight. There was always a party going on in Cloverdale on a Friday or Saturday night. If there wasn't a house party, there would be a party at Greenaway Pool and the park that surrounded it. Many of parties were thrown in baseball fields behind any of the many schools in town. We even partied at the graveyard. Kind of weird looking back. I guess that is what boredom creates. The mountains, ocean and city are too far away to get to by foot or skateboard, so let's go jump over bushes at the graveyard. This was our idea of fun.

Cloverdale is a small farming town. At least it was back at the time of these events. It was very rural and kind of isolated, located just a 45 minute drive away from Vancouver the largest metropolitan city in Western Canada. Any of the nearest neighboring cities between Cloverdale and the city were beyond walking distance and quite frankly not worth going to even if we had a ride. Leaving Cloverdale and going to parties in other municipalities usually meant fights. And for the most part, Cloverdale people were peaceful. We may have squabbles among our own, but it was usually just stupid stuff like fights over a girl or a couple of bozos who had too many drinks thumping their chests. There were rarely incidents involving gangs, guns, or real violence like we heard about from the larger surrounding cities. There really wasn't much going on in Cloverdale and because of that there also really wasn't much of a police presence. So, the youth could all congregate after hours in public places, and for the most part we all got along. It was a real mix of people too. Preps, jocks, punks, metalheads, G's, skateboarders, academic types, freaks, burnouts, we all meshed together on the weekends. The party tonight was on Ice Road. I'm not even sure if that is the actual name or if it is just what we had called it. Regardless, Ice Road was a narrow farm road rarely travelled in the evenings by anyone besides teenagers looking to get together. There were about 40 of us out that night. We had a big bonfire and plenty of drinks to go around. There was nothing remarkable about this get together. It was just standard weekend Cloverdale stuff. My friends picked me up. We stayed out drinking until late and then they drove me home. A typical Friday evening. A relatively quiet one if anything.

I woke up in my bed the next morning. I don't even remember how I got there. I know that I didn't drive which means one of my buddies that was drinking must've driven us all home that night. No one thought anything of it. It was just a classic Friday night, that's how it went. I had an appointment that morning at around 9:30am, and there was no way I was making that one. I don't know why I even scheduled one for that time, I should've known better, it was a weekend. But, that's how a lot of my life went, I just kind of lived in the moment and didn't think too far ahead. I had big day that day too. In hindsight, it's hard to comprehend how I had no clue just how life altering that day would prove to be.

That morning I was supposed to take my 1991 Chevy Cavalier Z24, my first car, down to the autobody shop because I was in a crash a few weeks before. That night, I had been out with buddies in downtown Vancouver and while driving across the Cambie Bridge I neglected to do a shoulder check while changing lanes. A car came flying up behind me and we clipped each other. Nobody was hurt, but both vehicles were minorly damaged. This was my third car crash to date, all of which had been my fault. Adrenaline, fearlessness and motor vehicles are a dangerous combination. A truth I would soon learn in the most severe of ways.

Anyway, I also had planned that day with Robyn. Robyn

was my high school sweetheart and the first love of my life. She came into the house that morning and woke me up. She was not too impressed that I was still sleeping and unmotivated to start our day together. The plan for the day was supposed to be that she was going to follow me down to drop my car off for repairs then I'd ride with her to an event. She was competing in a horse show that day, and it was a pretty big deal. Horses were Robyn's life and I enjoyed supporting her and being a part of that world. I spent many hours at her grandpa Fred's farm where she boarded her horses. There I would watch Robyn ride. I even hopped on her horse a couple of times, which gave me a huge respect for horse riders. I naively first looked at riding a horse from the mentality of a skateboarder. If I maneuvered my feet the right way I could make a skateboard do almost anything. Maneuvering a horse was an entirely different story, as a horse has a mind of its own. I learned quickly that I was better at horse watching than riding. So, if I were to do anything physical at the farm it would be help-ing out with chores like cleaning stalls, sweeping the barns or stacking hay bales. I was all in for Robyn's horseshow that Satur-day morning. That is until I stayed up partying into the wee hours the night before. I really didn't want to get out of bed, so Robyn left a bit angry and I rolled back over and went back to sleep. As for the missed appointment at the autobody shop, I figured worst case scenario I could easily just drop my car off another day. By the time I scraped myself out of bed it was nearly noon. I remember it being the perfect summertime morning. The sun shining warmly into my room, birds chirping and singing outside, and everything just felt ok. I mean, maybe a slight bit of drama because now I knew my girlfriend hated me for the moment, but this wasn't the first time I had been in the bad books for ripping it up with my friends and bailing on quality time with Robyn.

I quickly got myself together, hopped in my banged up car and drove down to the sandwich shop in town, Hansel Deli. Clo-verdale was just a little town, not very cosmopolitan by any means. The only shops on the street were a bar, a pawn shop, an old-time movie theatre, a small grocery store and half a dozen antique shops. Most of the faces of the people along the main street were recognizable. Quaint, little Cloverdale. My hometown. I pulled up to the deli, a ritual most weekend mornings. They were known for having these big monster sandwiches. A great remedy the day after a late night out. Being the caring boyfriend that I am, I thought in my infinite wisdom that I'd get an extra sandwich for Robyn as well. A peace offering to smooth things over.

Back in the car I headed off to Langley, the next community over and where Robyn was already in full competition mode. I believe Langley is the horse capital of the country... Or the world, I really don't know. Not sure how much credit you can give to titles places give to themselves. It's like everywhere I go ti eat has world famous garlic bread, but is it really world famous? Is it really?

I watched Robyn finish out her show while sitting with her family and friends. She was none too pleased with me. So, I kept a pretty low profile knowing I was guilty of being a crappy boyfriend and not wanting her to be any more upset with me than she already was. Robyn was in the zone that day. Must have been that sandwich I brought her. If only forgiveness were so easy to achieve. In the end, she kind of let it roll off as she has so many times before.

Robyn and I left her horseshow soon after it ended as we had plans to attend an event with my family starring (to us anyways) my youngest sister Hayley. Hayley was just five years old at the time, and she was set to perform in her first ever dance recital at the Langley School of Fine Arts later that night. This was not my first dance recital. No, I never danced myself. My fancy footwork was best performed on a skateboard, snowboarding, or with a pair of ice skates... these were my sports. Like Hayley, my sister Allison had been in dance from a young age. I had been to these recitals before. Never by choice. I remember putting up a fight every year that my parents would buy me a ticket to this annual event even though I see now it was a small sacrifice to make considering Allison attended years of hockey games and practices of mine. Yes, I was that pain in the butt older brother who gave his younger sister a hard time. I didn't want much to do with Allison as kids, even though now I can see she was the sweetest sister a big brother could have ever asked for and still is. Hayley and I had a different relationship growing up. I think it was owing mostly to the sixteen-year age gap between us. I assume it's pretty normal for siblings just a few years apart in age to bicker at each other. I didn't pick on Hayley in that way at all. When Hayley was really young if I took her to the park people assumed, she was my kid, and I think in some ways I looked at her that way so long as she didn't have a dirty diaper to be changed.

So, this was Hayley's big night. Her turn to strut her stuff onstage in front of a sold-out theatre of moms, dads, grandparents, sisters and reluctantly attending brothers. If any of you have younger siblings who dance, I'm sure you know all too well that these recitals are not the most organized of events. At least for the younger kids. Just a bunch of little humans, bumping around into each other, not really knowing what's going on, and proud parents looking on waiting for that moment when they see their kid up on stage so they can snap a photo. All the while hoping that their kid isn't the one who goes into meltdown mode and dismantles the entire routine. The kids have no idea what they're doing, but they're so excited to be there. So, you support them. We were a little wiser to this game and found out ahead of time when Hayley was going on stage, so Robyn, my Dad, Jim and I took it upon ourselves to go have a bite to eat at this place called, The Shark's Club not far from the theatre. After a bite and a drink, we went back just in time to see Hayley dance. It was cute and entertaining. Two of the kids got in a minor dispute over whose spot was who's on the dance floor, which was hysterical and probably the highlight of the night, besides watching my little sister. Afterwards I remember rushing over to Hayley and lifting her up above my head. My Dad gave her some flowers that he bought on the way, and yea, it was a happy evening. A special time for sure.

As we gathered outside to leave the recital I noticed a waxed-up curb along the sidewalk leading to the entrance of the theatre. There were a few other concrete structures I spotted that also looked like they would be fun to skate. I made a mental note. I HAVE to come back with my skateboard and shred this place. Never did I have the thought that soon enough, I wouldn't be skateboarding ever again. Robyn and I left together and headed to her trailer at the horseshow for some alone time. We officially made up here. This was also the last time I would be intimate with a girl with full use of my body. The day had turned out pretty great considering it's rocky beginnings. I didn't have any other plans for the night, every negative in my life had turned around and everything was better than ok, it was fantastic.

So, my plan from here was to go home, get some sleep and get up early. I had full intentions of having a mellow night and just chilling out. But then the phone rang. Apparently, there was a birthday party going on in Sullivan Station, a small suburb on the outskirts of town, but they did say it was a party. I'll be there. Famous last words.

I went to the garage and grabbed a couple of beers out of the fridge. Drank two or three of them just on the way to the party. Which was pretty much the norm. As I walked in, I saw a lot of familiar faces.

Growing up in Canada it's a huge hockey culture so I had played from a very young age as did a lot of the other guys in my school. So, I had a lot of friends just from playing hockey and the comradery of that over the years. I was pretty solid hockey player from a young age playing at the highest level with each year that I advanced. My dad lived and breathed hockey. Some of my oldest memories are of my dad on the couch in the living room in our old house on Aberdeen Street , TV full blast watching Hockey Night in Canada. My dad never had the opportunity to play such an expensive and time-consuming sport as hockey when he was a kid, so he was determined to provide his son with this opportunity. Hockey was pretty much my life from the time I could walk. Rumor has it that I was on ice skates even before I could walk. Also, that "Wayne Gretzky" were my first words. But, as I entered high school, I discovered another form of skating. This one being of the board. There are no pads in skateboarding, at least not when I was learning, and bails and slams were plentiful. Concrete is less forgiving than ice. I was often banged up and bruised and this was affecting my hockey performance. This along with my rebel without a cause attitude which was also in full affect at that time in my life made me a liability for my ice hockey team, the Cloverdale Colts. One practice I was really dragging my butt on the ice. My coach was not impressed and confronted me with an ultimatum. "Skateboarding or hockey." I didn't appreciate the way he stepped to me. I also identified myself more as a skateboarder than a hockey player. I didn't want to be a jock anymore. I wanted to be a punk. I didn't like anyone telling me what to do. There were no coaches in skateboarding. Just a bunch of hooligan friends who lived by their own terms. So, that's the short of it, I retired my ice skates for a skateboard and never really looked back. I did still have heart for the game of hockey though and a lot of buddies who still played it, but it just wasn't for me anymore. A lot of these buddies were at this party. I hadn't seen most of these familiar faces all together in a very long time. We were a team; we were used to seeing each other every day growing up. Road trips, championship games, we did it all together. These were my bro's. The party was on.

So, with the excitement of that, one beer led to two beers which ultimately led to five. Mind you, I already had two or three on the way here so I was well on my way to being intoxicated. The house was full of rowdy twenty-somethings getting their party on. Upstairs and downstairs. Front yard and backyard. In the kitchen, on the porch, in the hot tub. Fun times. I remember spotting Brendon in the hot tub surrounded by girls. Bren and my sister Allison had recently broken up. He seemed to be getting over it alright. Brendon and I grew up together on the ice. We mostly played on the same team every two years as he was a year younger than me. Our parents got along really well so we had done some long road trips together for tournaments and provincials. Bren was a cool kid. Quiet unless you got to know him. A sweet guy with a great sense of humor and a beast of a hockey player. Dude looked jacked in that hot tub. Hockey muscles were apparently stronger and more defined than skateboarding muscles. I had been mostly hanging at the party with a friend named Rob who I had known probably even longer than Brendon. Rob and I had had an ugly altercation some years before that had been instigated by me. Something I regretted. So, I was happy that on this night, Rob and I were hanging out and being bro's like the good old days. More recently, Brendon and I had also had a bit of an altercation right after he and Allison broke up. Nothing really major. Mostly just one heartbroken dude plus one protective big brother combined with testosterone alcohol and ego. Nothing physical. Just words between us. Similar to my feelings towards Rob that night, I imagine this might be why Brendon was eager to reconnect with me at this party. So, then there we were, just the three of us. And as parties go, this one started to wind down. Right around this time, word was going around of another even bigger party. So, the three of us and another buddy, Shane, all hopped in my car with no hesitation. Off we went. Finding the next party always seemed to be the mission of the night in these days and being at the next party was much more important than how we got to the party. Safety wasn't much of a concern. We were invincible. Kings of the world. Ok, Kings of Cloverdale. Just as we were about to leave, Rob's mom came outside and caught us. She told us, "Guys you know there's a case of beer in the car, you've already had enough to drink, you shouldn't be driving." But us being the bulletproof young men we thought we were, we blew her off. I told her it's fine I'm not drunk and won't be drinking anymore. A blatant lie.

Driving around Cloverdale, I drove fast. I liked to drive fast. The music was blaring. I liked loud music. We were all laughing and having a good time. Going around corners sideways, most would find this scary, but to us, it was fun. It was cool. Or so we thought. Lots of our friends had been in car crashes. Some of them serious. Many of them alcohol related. But nobody ever got seriously hurt. Nobody ever died.

We ended up down at a bar by the United States border, I believe it was called The Funky Planet. Inside the bar it was packed. There was some crappy dance music playing, not really my thing, but cheap drinks and pretty girls were enough of a distraction to block out the sound. The drinking age in Canada is 19 and 21 just across the line in the US. This meant tons of Americans made the trip into the great white North to get their first legal taste of alcohol. Scary to think how they all made it home. We didn't even give it a thought on this night. All focus was on the party and this place was going off. We ordered a few more beers and then started adding shots to the mix. We were drinking anything but responsibly. I, for one, was rather intoxicated by this point. The thrill of a packed bar with crappy music and first-time drinkers grew old. Rob knew of another party going on back in the heart of Cloverdale. With two parties too many under our belts already, we all piled into my car again and headed for another.

Again, I drove fast. Faster than usual. I took chances. More chances than usual. Just stupid. I made a quick pitstop back at home. As I pulled into the cul-de-sac, I turned the tunes down as to not wake up my dad. I shushed my buddies as I pulled into the driveway and stepped out of my car. I was drunk, but not the drunkest I had ever been I thought to myself as I typed the code into the garage door opener. I was on a mission. A stealth mission to get more alcohol. More beers for the me and the boys to bring to the next party. I found a 15 pack in the fridge. Score. Jim's going to be choked when he discovers them gone. I'll replace them tomorrow I reasoned with myself. He won't even know they were gone or that I came back home and went out again. But I'm sure my dad heard me enter the garage. He probably thought "Wow, Kevin is home kind of early for a Saturday night." I know he didn't expect to hear my car leave just moments later. He knew what I was up to and as I would later learn, he immediately began to worry. That sixth sense a parent has. The one kids don't like to pay attention to. That parental characteristic, most of us tend to just see as nagging. We dismiss the words when our parents call us on our own stupidity. Like they were never young? Like they don't know what we were actually doing? Or even scarier, what consequences can occur as a result of our careless decisions? The weird thing is that my dad was not the only one in that moment who had a strange feeling come over him. I too was struck with a feeling. A something. A voice of reason in my head that sounded like me. It sounded like me before drinking all those beers at the party and shots at the bar. "Just call it a night, Kevin. You have Robyn's horseshow tomorrow. If you party all night and sleep in again, she is going to kill you." The words reverberated clearly in my head as I stood in my driveway, box of beer in hand, looking at my car and back to my home and back to my car and my friends. "Maybe I should just go to bed." There was definitely a voice of reason and something telling me to just stop what I was doing. But I ignored it like I had so many other times. What's the worst that could happen? An angry dad? A disappointed girlfriend? I'd been there before.

After loading up, we made it to the next party. It was not far from my home and very close to my old high school. Sure, I knew people there, but it wasn't so much my normal crew of friends.Might as well just hang out with my buddies in the car. None of these signs that seem so clear in hindsight were visible that night though, unfortunately. This is starting to be where my story gets a little foggy.

I can't speak for the other guys in the car, but I had drank way too much by this point. My speech and mobility were impaired. Hours seem like seconds looking back. Faces all blend to-gether. What I do remember is it was a gorgeous summer night and this party was full of people. You go up the stairs, plenty of friends having fun, you go downstairs and there's more people. You would go outside and there's people just chilling on the lawn, just really happy people enjoying the summer night. Around this time my cell phone started to ring. Call after call from my mom and then my dad, my mom again and then my dad. They knew all too well what I was up to, but most concerning of all was that I had my car. My driving record was messy. Both of my parents who at this time were newly separated and not likely to agree with each other let alone communicate could definitely agree on one thing. My behavior. They were pleading with me to be smart and just call them for a ride home and not drive. A pretty sweet deal and pretty cool parental gesture if you stop and think about it. They were just looking out for me. "Have fun, but be safe " was the message. But I didn't see it that way. As a teenager or young adult, you kinda feel like they are "babying" you and you take it for granted but its honestly the greatest non-judgmental thing they can do. They would've given me a ride home. They would've given all my buddies a ride home. The calls kept coming in. I stopped answering. Kevin - Not a care in the world. My parents – sick to their stomachs with worry and fear.

Now, I don't know the circumstance the first time I tried to drive, but my friends had taken my keys away and hid them. I think they hid them in the back of the toilet which, by the way, is a great place to hide things should you ever need (I suggest this move to anyone looking out for friends at a party who may be in a state of mind to make such a poor decision as driving impaired. Just be sure to remove any electronics attached to said keys or else wrap everything in a couple of waterproof ziplocked bags to avoid permanent damage). But, what those good friends, who also were just looking out for me and anyone else on the road that night didn't know is that I kept a spare set of keys in my glove compartment. Jerk move. I stumbled to my car. It was only a five to eight-minute drive home. I could make it, I thought. I hopped in the car and started it up. Meanwhile my friends, Rob, Brendon and Shane had actually called a taxi to get us all home safely. Good for them. But not for me. I wanted to drive. They were trying to get me to come with them. They knew I shouldn't be driving. Everyone did. Unfortunately, at that point, I was past any voice of reason in my own head or anyone else's. It was like I had something to prove. I was that guy. The guy who always had to take things to the next level. The guy who would touch the hot dinner plate after being warned it was hot. But I would just touch the plate. I would grasp it in my hands and grit my teeth and show everyone just how hardcore I could be as it scolded my skin. The taxi arrived and one by one Rob, Brendon and Shane teetered their way in. I sat in my car as the engine warmed shuffling through my CD case looking for the ideal punk rock anthem for my short ride home. Punk rock songs are short. I would only need one or two to get me home to my bed in one piece. Hungover or not I would wake up in the morning and deal with how haggard I felt and make it to Robyn's horse show. Another fun weekend. The start of what was going to be a summer to remember. Suddenly, my passenger door flies open. It's Brendon. He's getting in with me. He's not taking the taxi either. I don't think there was any question at this point that either of us wanted to go home. We were going to keep this party going. Brendon knew a place to go. Perfect, I thought. It was only 1am or so at this point. The night was still young. I remember saying to Brendon "Buckle up." The one good driving habit I had at that point in my life. I always wore my seatbelt and asked the same of my friends. Considering the way I drove, this was a no brainer. Probably the only good choice I made that night, Brendon and I both buckled up for the ride.

With Brendon in my passenger seat I backed out of the driveway. A couple of buddies on a mission. Our destination - more fun. Kind of like when we were kids on the ice. Teammates working for a common goal. Get to the other end of the ice as fast as we could in one piece. The reward - a goal. The goal this night was another party. We drove past our old high school on the right. We drove past Greenaway Hill where we used to have snowball fights in the winter and play frisbee in the summer. I barreled down 180th St towards #10 Hwy. A red light. We're stopped. "Bro Hymn" by Pennywise was blasting on my stereo. The irony of this, the song is a tribute to friends of the band who died young. Brendon loved this song and always made me play it when we were out together. I loved it too and was stoked that he loved it. We are happy. We are singing *"Wooooh. Ohhh. Ohhh. Ohhhhh... To all my friends present, past and beyond. To all of those who weren't with us too long. Life is the most precious thing you can lose"*...

This is my last memory.

At the red light, we had a choice to make. Do we turn right and go home? Or turn left and continue the partying? It's these moments that you should always take the safer road if you're met at this fork in life. I should've gone right. I wished I had gone right. I wish I had never drove at all. But I didn't go right. Buckle up... because here we go.

I turned left, and tires squealing peeled off down the road. Heading out of Cloverdale towards Langley I was heading up the hill to an intersection at 192nd street. It was a pretty busy intersection, with a pretty mellow corner up ahead. The corner was nothing new to me, I had driven this road hundreds of times whether leaving work or a buddy's place. It was a road I was very familiar with. Aside from that it was a clear night, and no one else was on the road. I drove this road all the time, and I've driven it fast, often without worry. But I don't remember any of this. From what I know, I hit a road divider. There's a small divider in between the exit and entry and it's a very small curb, but when you're going as fast as I was that small curb launched my car into the air. At that point - it's all over. You couldn't regain control if you wanted to. It hit the ground nose first and began to roll multiple times end over end. Flinging us helplessly all around. Flipping and rolling. Shattering and crunching the car like an aluminum can caught in a strong wind. My car finally stops upside down wedged into a small embankment cut into a grassy patch between the highway on the left and a parking lot and store fronts to the right. A stretch of grass that had never meant anything to me before. I never could have imagined that night or any night before that this would be the spot where so many lives would be forever changed.

Across the street was a Ramada Hotel and as luck would have it, due to vehicle break in's being common in the area at the time, employees were asked to be more alert to noises. Fortunately, an employee that night heard the breaking glass from the crash. He went into the parking lot to confront the "thieves' and as he did, across the street he could see my taillights glowing in the dark and smoke rising. The squeal of a tortured engine idling in full gear, struggling not to choke out.

He immediately called 911, and first responders were there in minutes. The car crashed so violently that the wheels came off, and a rim flew across the field and stuck into the side of a nearby building. It was a high impact crash site. Littered with CD's, clothing, blood and glass everywhere. It literally looked like a bomb went off inside the vehicle. We flipped and turned and rolled, every time we did the metal in the car coffin-ed us in. When we finally stopped, we were upside down in a ditch at the lower end of the field. We were both unconscious and upside down held in only by our seatbelts. Blood and motor fluids filled the cabin of the Cavalier. I was told later that had I not had my seatbelt on, the fluid buildup would've flooded my lungs and I would've drowned before paramedics would even have arrived on scene.

The compaction of the car made it extremely difficult for first responders to even get us out of the car. We were both in very rough shape, both had head traumas and excessive bleeding. The only way to get Brendon out of the car was to go over me. Not only had I put Brendon in this life or death situation, but now I also ended up blocking the paramedics from even being able to properly reach him. They had to get me out first. There was no other way and there was very little time for either of us. It was that bad. Seatbelts or no seatbelts when you hit the ground with that kind of speed and force the impact is devastating. Later in the book you will see photos and you can get a clear idea of how devastating it was to my car. An impact like this crushes, tears and mangles the steel. Imagine what it does to flesh, skin and bone. I feel horrible even for what I put these paramedics through. One of them was our family friend, Gwen and the other, Denise, whom I met many years later, paradoxically after sharing this very story at her son's high school. We would meet again, and I would learn details that I do not remember seeing, hearing or feeling that night. Details I would never want to see or remember. Details I will not share here out of respect for Brendon's family. Details nobody should ever have to hear, see or feel. Details nobody would ever want to inflict upon themselves or worse yet on others. Heartbreaking, devastating, life altering and life ending details. So many lives were forever changed that night. Not just Brendon's and mine, but our families' and friends'. Even the paramedics who were on scene that night. Denise being a mom herself. She was there doing her job. It seemed like a routine call at first if there is such a thing for a first responder. But this was not like any call or worse yet, any scene she had ever seen before. These were two young men. They could have been boys for all she knew. We could have been her boys. Her boys who were safe at home in bed. Her boys who she would go home and hug tightly with tears in her eyes at the end of her shift. Her job that night was to try and save the lives of these boys. But those boys were us. Boys that wanted to give our mothers that chance to hug us one more time and tell us they loved us. But we couldn't do that. Not that night. The paramedics didn't have time to save both of us, so they had to choose who had the best likelihood of survival. And they had to make that choice that night. Who's going to live? And this was extremely unfair of me to put on them, this was all my fault. And it's the first of many guilts I live with to this day.

Two young guys in this vehicle and this woman who is a mother to her own small boys. Note to everyone: All mothers always see their sons as young boys no matter how old we get. You'll always be her little boy. So that's what she saw that night. Two helpless boys, dying. A testament to how awful the situation was, paramedic Gwen, being a family friend didn't even recognize me due to how badly I was mangled in the wreckage. I didn't recognize Gwen either. I had no idea she was there. I had no idea I was there. All I remember if I can even use the word remember is darkness. There was nothing. One second was happiness, music, joy, fun times with my buddy ... And then the lights turned out. Darkness. Nothing.

Years later, my buddy Rob told me that their taxi went right by the crash site. Whether it was the fact that my car was unrecognizable or his own sizable intake of alcohol that night, it never dawned on Rob that it might have been us in the wreck. Imagine that, the guys who were stuck waiting for a cab, just slow and steady made it to their destination. Four guys out partying. Two of us made a bad choice. Two of us made a good choice. The good choice cost maybe $10.00. The bad choice cost us everything.

I was rushed to Royal Columbian Hospital with life threatening injuries. My injuries included a head injury, losing a ton of blood, and a collapsed lung. The collapsed lung actually had the greatest chance of killing me. I don't think they even knew yet that I was paralyzed.

Then, every parent's nightmare happened. My parents' phone rang. My mother works for RCMP the Royal Canadian Mounted Police, so she actually knew the policeman who eventually showed up to her place. Her first words were "Is he alive?" They told her she just needs to "come with them." They said I was "alive, but probably not for much longer." I don't know how Brendon's family received the worst news of their lives. It's not something I feel comfortable asking them. I can only imagine everything that they went through from their first interaction with the police until this day. Even my own family and friends seldom talk about the minutes, hours and weeks that immediately followed their knowledge of the crash. Nearly twenty years later the memories are still so painful that we can barely speak of them with one another. We don't pretend not to know what happened, we all know what happened. It's just too hard to go back to those moments together. Many of what you are about to read in the pages ahead, I also just read for the very first time. I never even knew these details. Just a heads up. You might want to grab some Kleenex.

2

Ingrid: A Parent's Worst Fear

"He got very agitated and he said, "Tell me why I can't move my legs." I told him "Kevin, you're paralyzed." And we sat there in silence"

I don't think any parent is ever prepared for when they get that dreadful knock at the door. I got that knock at just after 5am on June 24th, 2000. Kevin's younger sister, Hayley had her ballet recital earlier in the evening and his sister Allison had her commencement ceremony the night before. It was a great couple of days for our family. I had the night off, but would be back at work at the Surrey RCMP the next morning where I am a police dispatcher.

So, when I got home that night, I knew Kevin was already going to be going out. It wasn't anything unusual just another normal summer night. At around 1am in the morning my phone rang, I looked over and it was Kevin's dad, Jim. I picked up the phone and he asked if I had talked to Kevin. I told him I have not. He then told me how he had been fast asleep but awoke to the garage door opening. Apparently, Kevin had come in to grab some beers and left again. Jim tried to stop him, but by the time he reached the garage Kevin was already gone. Jim had a bad feeling about the night.

Jim had called me because he reached out to Kevin multiple

times and his phone calls all went unanswered. It was the same for me. I called a few times and it went right to voicemail. Which only means he either turned off his phone or was ignoring me. Now I was worried. I laid in bed and couldn't fall asleep after that. Parents will always worry about their children no matter how old they get. I tossed and turned hour after hour. The phone was still in my hand when I got the intercom buzz at 5am.

At around 3am I awoke to sirens. Not one, but multiple. It was not only police but also ambulance and fire. It was definitely something serious for all units to be called in, and it was right outside my window. In an instant, I thought to myself, "This is bad." I had a gut wrenching thought that this was all for Kevin. I fought this thought as much as I could, but I couldn't. I knew in my heart that something had happened to him. I had a horrible, horrible feeling in the pit of my stomach. I tried calling him again. Voicemail. And then it happened. My life changed forever.

My buzzer rang at 5am. I didn't need to look out the window, I already knew. I answered the intercom and it was Heather, a police officer that I work with. Before I could get any words out, Heather spoke and said "Ingrid, you need to let me in." I froze up for a moment and then bluntly asked her, "Just tell me. Is he dead or alive?" She seemed surprised by my words, but I know how this works. If the police show up to your door, the chances are someone has died. If not, you generally will get a phone call. I continued on and told her "I can't let you up here until you can tell me whether Kevin is dead or alive. In order to be able to face you, I need to know up front what I'm dealing with." She asked if I already had heard some information. I told her "no", but that those sirens were definitely something serious and it had to do with Kevin. Heather sighed and told me that Kevin had been critically injured in a car crash, but that he was alive... For now. I immediately went downstairs to meet her.

I don't remember the drive to the hospital, I remember asking if anyone spoke to Jim yet and told him what had happened. She said "Someone was on their way to way to his house as well." Jim was outside when we got there and we walked into the emergency room together. There, on the bed, barely recognizable, laid Kevin. He had tubes in and out of his body, doctors working frantically all around him. His face was twice the size. Part of his lip was hanging off just above his chin. It looked like someone had taken a hatchet to his arm. I checked the clock, it was 6:00am, June the 24th. I stood over his bed, trying not to get in the way. Fighting back tears, I just wanted to touch him, to hug him and tell him "I love him."

Eventually, a doctor came over and took Jim and I aside. He solemnly said, "We needed to speak." He began with "Kevin has about a 40% chance of surviving. He's in critical condition and there are concerns regarding his reflex responses." When I asked him to explain, he plainly said "His lower body extremities are not responding to stimuli. They would be monitoring him closely." We then stepped out of the room, I'm not sure how long I had been holding my breath.

Heather was still in the hospital. She came over to me and told me she needed to speak to me privately. They had identified the passenger in Kevins car. It was Brendon.

I remembered Brendon from dating my daughter Allison, and that he grew up playing hockey with Kevin for years. He was a great kid, and it just didn't even register for me at that moment that he was gone. I just kept thinking about his mom and dad. In one room my son is fighting for his life, and in another room a family is grieving the loss of their son. As I went in and out of the emergency room, I saw a large group of Kevin's friends in the waiting area. They all heard what had happened and rushed right over. They wanted to see him, but no one was allowed in. They kept asking me, "Is he going to make it?" I had no answers, I had to look them in the face and all I could say was "I don't know. All we can do is hope and pray." A few hours passed and he was moved into the isolation ward. Allison and I would stand on either side of him and just repeat over and over "Kevin, can you hear us? If you can hear us blink your eyes." We held his hand; he didn't hold it back. We repeated it again and again. And then – He blinked his eyes one time. He didn't have the strength to keep them open, but he heard us.

It was Friday, June 30th, the start of the Canada Day long weekend. The specialist was meeting with me that afternoon to apprise me of Kevin's prognosis. I was sitting with a friend in the cafeteria when I spotted him. He was with his daughter. In less than 30 seconds he had introduced himself and delivered the words that changed our lives forever. He said that Kevin had an incomplete spinal cord injury and was paralyzed from the chest down. He went on to say that he would be transferring from this hospital tomorrow to a spinal cord unit at Vancouver General Hospital. And then he started to walk away. I stood in front of him, stunned & shocked that he was so laissez-faire about it. I said, "what does that mean? I don't know what you're saying, what is incomplete?" He blankly responded , "Spinal cord severs are very rare. Think of it like this, its like toothpaste, you push down on it and it makes a dent. The dent remains. That is your son's spine." He went on to say that Kevin would never walk again. Then he went on to tell me how he had weekend plans and would be leaving for the holiday with his family. I stood there absolutely stunned and felt my world spinning around me. My friend came over and hugged me. I couldn't talk. I was not expecting those words. This time I couldn't stop the tears.

The next day was Brendon's funeral and I wasn't prepared for that. How do we go to a funeral for a boy who passed away and the person responsible for his death was my own son? At the funeral words were spoken to pray for Kevin's recovery. When the service was over, I left right away. I went to the hospital and watched as they loaded Kevin and moved him to another very cold hospital, VGH. I remember the air conditioning blowing very cold air on Kevin's bed, and with limited hospital staff over the holiday weekend I just laid there with him wanting him to be warm. I was wrestling with the pain of him being in so much pain himself. This is where he would spend his first 5 weeks, on the 9th floor, in isolation.

His two months at Vancouver General had started. I stayed at the hospital every single day, and slowly I saw him start to come around. He had a trach in his throat and was unable to speak so I spent the next few months learning to read lips, so I had some way to communicate with him. When he started to gain a little strength he would use a pencil and scribble on paper to talk to me. We didn't talk about the car crash; he would only speak of random things mostly due to the drugs he was medicated with. He still thought his car was at the 7-11 down the street. He asked if I had his keys and could go get it, I would tell him "of course I would." I went along with most of the conversations to keep him comfortable. As the medications changed, he would become more lucid and more aware. He still didn't know what day it was, but he never asked why he was in the hospital. I was afraid of what would happen when he did ask what happened to him. It was about three to four weeks later when he did ask me. I was all alone at the time, and he mouthed the words "Mom, why can't I move my legs?" I felt crushed on the inside and I couldn't avoid the truth any longer. I said "Kevin, you have a spinal cord injury." He got very agitated and he said, "Tell me why I can't move my legs." I told him "Kevin, you're paralyzed." And we sat there in silence.

When I said those words he just laid very still. It was just absolutely quiet and I never fought so hard to hold back my tears. He had four tubes in his chest, a tube in his throat, his legs didn't move, and he was so very pale all over. It took a few minutes to sink in, but then he asked, "Was anyone in the car with me?" I told him "yes." He began guessing names. Every time he said a name I would answer "No." When I told him it was Brendon, he asked "Where is he?" I didn't know how to say the next few words. I held his hand and just said it. "Kevin, Brendon is dead." It was then, for the first time, that I saw Kevin, totally and completely break down.

To watch my 21-year-old son, in a hospital bed, cry like I've never seen before and unable to wipe his own tears, not able to get up, not able to walk away or even scream and ask himself why. We both cried for a very long time. I know what he was thinking after as he said many times in his presentations, and I know what a devastating blow it was to hear both of those things in one instant. It was on that day that everything changed in the hospital for us.

He had the best care possible; he was directly across from the nurse's station, the staff loved him, but his body was broken and no loving care could fix that. As he learned this news, I didn't know if he would ever be the same person again emotionally. In the coming weeks he was able to start to have visitors. They were few at first, and I would be sure to screen people as they came in. As he got stronger there were exercises that he would need including breathing on his own. It was extremely painful for me to watch, for every one or two breaths he would need to be plugged back into the machine to keep him going. He was transferred to another room, and I didn't realize how lifeless he was until that day.

The nurses arrived with a contraption that held a giant sling that went under his back, under his arms, under each leg and strapped him in like a diaper. Then, from behind, lifted him. They needed to crank the sling to lift him off the bed. When I saw him in that sling, from the chest down everything lifeless, everything hanging and his body being frail and broken he told them he felt dizzy. They needed to remove him and place him back in the bed. I walked out of the room, back against the wall and I just crumpled to the ground. I was shattered. I knew I had to pull myself together, for him. Things are definitely going to be different now. Not all things, but I'm going to have to accept and move forward.

Kevin stayed there another few months. On one of our visits we found out that Kevin had been moved to a critical isolation ward. We noticed his friend Geoff sitting on a chair nearby. Geoff looked upset and couldn't muster any words. But that's when we heard something else. Something we haven't heard in what felt like forever. As we walked into the room, we heard, "Hey mom. Hi Hayley." I looked back at Geoff and his smile was ear to ear. It had been 7 weeks since I heard my son's voice. And now, here we are. Speaking. I can have a conversation with my son, without the aid of machinery. It was no nice to hear his voice again.

A few weeks later, Kevin was moved again. This time to GF Strong rehab facility. We looked forward to the next stage of recovery, but I was scared. We held a "Getting Better" celebratory gathering with friends, even though he wasn't out of the woods just yet. We brought balloons and put them next to his bed and noticed an empty bed next to his, apparently Kevin was going to be having a roommate. We went down to the car and as we came back, we saw another young man, early 20's wheeling himself out of the room in a wheelchair. And he turned to us and said, "Are you the ones who left those fucking balloons in my room?" I wasn't expecting that. I said "Yes, I'm Kevin's mom and I thought it would brighten the room a bit." He turned his back and as he began wheeling away spouted "Well isn't that fucking lovely?" I didn't know what to say. So, I walked to the office and asked if this was his roommate by choice or default. They told me that the doctors try, and match roommates based on personality. This guy was matched with Kevin. At first I thought, there must be a mistake they're nothing alike. Then the nurses told me, because Kevin is so positive they had hoped by sharing a room with him, he could help this other boy. This made me smile.

Everyone has their own sad story. And in the end, the two became friends as roommates and as having that common bond. This guy had more emotional stuff going on in his life, and just needed to talk. Kevin listens. He listens when people need to talk and sometimes it's just something as simple as needing to just get it all out. This guy was on his own, he was estranged from his family, and only had one other friend. So, Kevin being there, and just being a friend to him when no one else would, meant the world to him. And you don't know everyone's story, you don't know why they are the way they are unless you ask. So sometimes it is a good idea to just reach out and ask people ya know?

As summer days faded away, turning into fall, and fall became winter, we had hoped Kevin would be able to come home by Christmas but knew it may not be possible. He was getting day passes which meant he could come home for weekends but would always have to go back to rehab that following Monday. It was always a struggle when he did come home, the house we had sold, and I was living in a small apartment at the time. It was tight and squishy, and didn't have the best wheelchair access, but we made it work.

It was around Halloween that Kevin came home on a day pass and he was going to go to a Halloween party, but he didn't know what he was going to be. So, I thought, why don't you go as Superman. Christopher Reeves who played Superman in the 1980's movies had been in an accident recently as well and he was in a wheelchair. So, both of them were Clark Kent in a wheelchair and Superman outside of it. So, I went to the store and rented him the costume. In my mind, it seemed like an amazing idea but what I failed to realize is that that costume is skintight. Kevin had a hard-enough time just putting on pants how am I going to squeeze him into blue tights? I can only compare this action to say a baby when you're trying to dress them and you can't tell them "Point your toe" so you can squeeze it through. He can't point his toe, so you have to do each and every little nuance of movement to get him in there. And that's what it was like. He couldn't even lift himself off the bed. It was a real ordeal, but we finally got him into his outfit then his sister and her boyfriend came and took him to this party. I thought, this is great. Life carries on. He's going to adjust alright now. Life is good. And that kind of backfired.

People at the party thought that he was being a jerk and mocking Christopher Reeves for being in a wheelchair. It wasn't until Kevin looked at them and said, "Well I can't walk either, man" that they understood. He came home late that night and I heard the door open. His sister had already left, and I had fallen asleep earlier but awoke when he came in. I normally hear the wheels rolling on the floor as he would make his way to his room or the kitchen. So, I got up and I looked from the doorway, he didn't even know I was there, but I saw him. Alone. In the corner, he just sat in his wheelchair crying. It was an absolutely gut-wrenching moment for me as a mom. I thought, some superhero idea I had. What a mistake. I went over and hugged him, and he told me how people thought he was a real jerk for mocking Superman, and it really darkened his evening. So, the lesson there is there will always be things you find funny, that others won't. All you can do is try to make the best of a bad situation, but sometimes even that can backfire, but you get up and keep moving.

On the 17th of December we got our Christmas wish and Kevin came home. It was the best day ever. It was a hard day at the same time. I remember wheeling him in and thinking, "How are we going to manage? Really? There's just not enough room." He had an occupational therapist come in and take measurements to make sure that everything would be conducive to his needs, whether it be getting to the kitchen or the bathroom to just fitting through door frames with the chair. It turned out he JUST fit.

We managed to get him his own room. I took my bedroom and made it Kevin's room. I moved everything of mine out and into Hayley's room where I would share a room with my daughter for the next two years. This is where life is, this is where it starts. We are starting our life over, and that's exactly what we did. The first few months were difficult. That winter, we don't typically get a lot of snow around our home, but we get some. However, it did snow in the mountains and we would always go skiing together, it was a family tradition. But I remember I awoke one morning, and I could see through the bathroom window that it was snowing. As I made my way to the living room, I noticed that Kevin had wheeled himself to the patio door and was just watching the snow fall. I could only see the back of him as he watched the white flurries pile up. And I didn't even need to see his face to know, he was crying just watching it fall. Knowing he would never snowboard with us again. And at that point I told myself, I'm never going to ski again either. I wouldn't mention it to him, but from that moment onward I just wouldn't go. I couldn't enjoy something without him there, and if he couldn't go then neither would I.

Two winters had passed when he finally asked me why I didn't go skiing anymore. And I lied and told him it was because I was getting older, I was afraid to break a bone or get injured. He looked me dead in the eye and called my lie. He said, "You're lying. That's not why you're not going, I don't believe you, you love skiing. You taught us all how to ski. It's your favorite thing to do. It's YOUR thing! You can't stop doing what you enjoy doing just because I can't." So, that next year, I found myself back on the slopes. And he taught me not to feel bad about it. Just because you get knocked down doesn't mean you can't get back up again, and that's how he lives his life and I think that's how all of us live our lives now because of him. You only have one life, and you're entitled to have bad days its fine. But you know what? Just stop your crying. There's nothing wrong with feeling sorry for yourself, but just don't do it all the time. You have the choice to make life different. It's all up to you. You all have family and friends, and hopefully an able body that can take you places. So, there's so much to be thankful for. And you can have bad days, I've had some really awful ones, but you know what? It'll happen. You just can't let it drag you down for too long.

A few months later I was having lunch with friends I haven't seen in over ten years. And living in a small community everyone knows the news of what happened. But I was sitting at lunch with them and they were trying to be so supportive and they all knew about Kevin doing his school presentations, or have seen him on the news, or read about him and I know what they're about to say. I bite my tongue. And I'll preface it with, I know they MEAN the best, but they'll say to me "You know if it was going to happen to anybody Kevin has the personality to overcome it, so it's good that its him." I know they are trying to be nice. But... You have no idea. No idea. June 23rd, 2000, I wish to God I had gotten a hold of him on those telephone calls that night. Nineteen years have passed and what I wouldn't do to bring that night back and change it for him. Nineteen years of birthdays. He watched his younger sister make a wish on her birthday and for nineteen years. Do you know the only thing Hayley wished for? We did. It was for Kevin to walk again.

A few years after the crash, I was in my room when I heard a banging noise. I got up and saw Hayley in Kevin's wheelchair. She was fumbling around the apartment with it. She tried to take it into the bathroom, at this point she must've been about seven or eight years old, but she told me she wanted to know what it felt like. I said, ok as long as Kevin didn't mind. And I watched as she backed it in and maneuvered it, and anytime she made a mistake and put her foot down she would start the entire process over again. And at seven years old, I was so impressed with her wanting to understand. When Kevin went to swim therapy, Hayley and I would get in the pool with him. We would try to only use our arms in the water. Believe me, it's not easy.

Nineteen years later, when people say, "He took something so bad and turned it into something so good." I don't even hear the words anymore. It used to bother me, but now I've just heard it so many times. As a parent, you don't know how I wish it was June 23rd again and we were at Hayley's recital. I would've given

Kevin a ride to that party, and to the next one and to the next if he wanted. It doesn't matter. That's what goes into my mind. There will always be people who get into cars drunk, there will always be people who ride with drunk drivers and I work for the Royal Canadian Mounted Police, so I hear those stories. And I didn't know how I'd be able to adjust going back to work and hearing more of those stories.

People don't understand the implications, it's never just "you" that gets hurt should something go wrong. You destroy lives, multiple lives. Entire families' lives. Forget about just yourself for a minute and think about your parents, your friends, your friends' parents. Think about that stranger and their family if your stupidity crashed into an innocent person just driving home and killed them. It's so stupid. One thing about Kevin that night, I'm glad he wore a seatbelt. It doesn't guarantee safety, but you have a much better chance of survival. Even if you are going to be stupid, be smart enough to do that. I'll hear these stories and swear up and down at the stupidity of drunk drivers. Kevin was one of them. But now, he makes his life all about helping people.

Aside from doing his speeches, he answers every single message that kids send him whether it's on Facebook, or Instagram or emails. And he keeps all of them. He genuinely cares about each and every one of the kids that reach out to him. It's who he is. It's who he was before the car crash and it's still who he is now, and I couldn't be prouder of him. I am so proud of my son every day. As much as he may get under my skin, because he can, or as cocky as he is at times as much as he can be a bad ass, he just has such a loving personality. Whenever we have family dinners people ask, "When is Kevin getting here?" He's just that entertainer. He has that electric personality that you want to be around him. I couldn't imagine not having him here. He's a grown man now, and he's independent, I love that he's independent we've been through a lot together. He is not only my son but he's also my friend. \Do we know each other inside out? No. Should we know each other inside out? No. You just accept and love those close to you and cherish the time you have with them. But whenever people come up to me and tell me anything about him, I really can't help but smile and think, yup, that's my kid. And I'm so proud of him. I'm so, so, so very proud to be his mom.

3

Allison: My Brother, My Hero

"Every time we are together, we see it, whether we want to or not. Our lives are permanently altered."

When I see my brother on the news, it brings back a lot of sad memories. Seeing my brother in a wheelchair has never been easy and I still can't get used to seeing it. I've known him for 18 years without a chair, and I know a lot of time has passed but it's still hard to see. I'm sure he feels it every day. Every time I see him, I know it hurts him to know that he can't walk. So, even at times it still hurts to see him speaking in public or being interviewed it tends to be bittersweet. I know what he's doing, he's doing for a reason and for a greater good and that he's helping people. A lot of people. But to me, he's my big brother. He used to chase me around the house and dunk me in the lake. Typical things that all siblings do.

My proudest moments with Kevin, would be seeing him speak to kids. Having worked with kids myself over the past twenty years I know exactly how they are and how long their attention spans can last So, when someone like him comes along and captures their mind, it's really impressive. He's relatable, he's real, and he never portrays to be anything that he's not. Just the genuine dude you meet, and he is that way to everyone who crosses paths with him. This is also why he's so effective at helping them.

I tried to think of a dark moment for this book. Something that could really hit home and make kids understand that life is precious, and that it isn't a game to be risked on stupid behavior. Well, I couldn't think of one dark moment, because there are far too many of them. But I will speak in general of times that hit him the most. Losing the ability to do basic things whether it's around the home or out in public, Kevin gets extremely frustrated. He never will say anything though, he doesn't ask for help and doesn't want you to fawn all over him, but it's the look in his eyes and you just know. A piece of you cries when this happens. To see your big brother, your protector and instigator at times completely helpless and staring back at you from a chair is heartbreaking. Especially when it's over something so seemingly simple like putting on a shoe or a sock. Another issue that's common in Vancouver, anytime we would be outside and it started to rain, we all run for cover. Kevin can't run for cover. He has to wheel himself as best he can, find a ramp, and then hopefully get under some kind of shelter. By that time he's soaking wet. These moments hurt. They really hurt. He's always a few steps behind us in those circumstances.

After he was recovering when he came home from the hospital, I knew he was very depressed over Brendon. There were days he wouldn't leave the house. He stayed in his room blasting music and not speaking to anyone. These were the toughest. Because you want to help, but he just doesn't let you in. These are things now I know that I could just sit there in silence with him and sometimes for those going through sadness they just need that company. So that way they don't feel so alone.

Another difficult time for him was at the beach. He would sit on the sand and stare out at the ocean. I knew exactly what he was feeling. I'm never going to walk on that sand again or touch my toes to the water. Again, such simple acts that most of us don't even bother doing, and for Kevin, he would give anything ANY-

THING to feel the sand squish between his toes or the cold water running over them as the waves come in and out. But he feels nothing. And never will again. He can only watch with his eyes and remember.

Living in Canada, I'm close to the mountains and a family tradition we have is skiing. My mom taught us all how, but Kev preferred to go snowboarding. Again, something he'll never do again. He loved snowboarding. Skating and snowboarding you really couldn't keep him from either. They were his passions, it's all he talked about. And like in his speech "Imagine you couldn't just grab your board and skate anymore...", that is exactly it. Imagine taking away the one thing that made you passionate and were told you just can't do it anymore. For no other reason except you just aren't allowed to anymore. What if you were an artist and someone asked you to help paint their bedroom? Nope. Can't do it. Not allowed to touch a paintbrush ever again. Or what if you were a singer and you just weren't allowed to talk anymore? These examples seem ridiculous but this is how it is for Kevin. He loved being outdoors, he loved to skate and snowboard but his legs just won't let him and he never had a chance to slowly let that adjust for him. That decision was made for him in a matter of seconds. Never again.

There's a lot of things though that he'll never do again. Kevin told me the time he downloaded a dating app on his phone. He chose his best pictures, his wittiest lines, (and he is a witty guy let's face it he's downright hysterical at times) and he's a good-looking man. He started racking up matches immediately. Feeling confident, feeling good, feeling wanted and desired he went out on a date. Things went well at first, some of his girlfriends actually lasted for quite some time, but in the end it always turned out the same - he was alone. By no fault of his, it was just the situation. The chair became too hard for them for get over. And I felt bad for my brother, because for a time he was happy and things just always seem to turn sour. I think it had to do with the fact when they started thinking long term they just weren't comfortable with "How would Kevin take care of me when we're older?" It was as if they didn't see him as a fully capable man, even though he is more capable than most men I know, but they just couldn't see it. And it hurt my brother, but like anything else he just moves on. He tries to be happy and pretend it doesn't bother him, but deep down I know it does. No one wants to be alone. It became too much of an emotional blow every time. Granted he has met some stellar women and gone on a few dates, but it's never been easy. Not now.

The only thing that makes it harder is our sense of family. I know Kevin wanted to get married and have kids one day, and now he sees his younger sister married with children before him. And he'll see his baby sister married with children before him. He'll never be able to have kids of his own. And THAT is something that really affects him. It's probably why he does what he does. He treats the kids in the schools as if they were his own. He genuinely cares, and only wants the best for them. Even if they're being the typical adolescents, like any parent would, he just wishes them the best.

Now in telling you the things he'll never do again, I'll tell you the things myself and my friends and most of the community we associate with has never done again. We never drank and drove again. It was a typical thing to do, so no one blames Kevin for being foolish, kids are kids, they make stupid decisions. To say that you will never drink and drive or be just over the limit and get behind the wheel would be a lie, most everyone does at one point. Sometimes you really think you are just fine but that half a beer extra you consumed is enough to slow your judgement down half a second. And that half a second could be the difference. With Kevin, just grazing that curb was a half second adjustment before losing control. At that point it's not up to you. But the steps leading up to that are totally up to you. My friends and I never drank and drove again. We know far too well the consequences. And not just from knowing Kevin. Every time we are together, we see it, whether we want to or not. It affects all of us.

4

Geoff: Best Buds, Possessed to Skate

"I honestly don't like talking about this, it brings up too many bad memories and gets me choked up every single time."

I was with Kevin earlier that day just skating as we always would do, just skating and hanging out. I decided not to go out that night because I was too tired to go out to another party. I didn't even know he was going to his sister's grad party and it wasn't until later that night that I got the phone call at the house. I don't remember who called that night, I've blocked a bit of the memory out as much as I could. I do know when I did get to the hospital that night, I was told Kevin had a 10% chance to live and I needed to say goodbye. I walked in the room and saw him, completely unrecognizable, he looked like the Marshmallow Man. For the next several hours we waited at the hospital not knowing what was going to happen, and I just remember being so scared I was going to lose my friend. He was my best friend.

Growing up skating together, he was my hype man, my right corner. As I started getting sponsorships, Kevin was always there building me up and cheering me on. He was the closest person to me in my life. The aftermath was gnarly to say the least. It was life changing for everyone. After he started to recuperate, I would continue skating but the trips to the skate park became less and less. And I was never the same again. The joy of skating was gone from my life. I fell into a bit of depression and couldn't leave the house.

There were days where I didn't even want to get out of bed. The whole ordeal threw my life into a bit of a downward spiral. The biggest thing was, if anyone in the world could be in that situation it would be him. He is the only person I know who is strong enough, and I honestly don't like talking about this, it brings up too many bad memories and gets me choked up every single time. Everything that we did, and I mean everything, changed forever. He keeps his depression hidden from everyone and he kept trying to cheer everyone else up, and that was super difficult to see. We knew what was really going on for him.

Having to pick him up and put him into a car the very first time was hard to watch. We didn't know what to do, and we would be trying with everything we had in us to lift him up. Watching him struggle as he sits there helpless, it's just not the friend I knew. But we tried to get over it and move on as if nothing had happened. We would sneak him out of the hospital and take him to punk shows and bring him back before anyone noticed.

Kevin was and still is one of the craziest people I know. If he still had two legs, who knows where he would be today, I'm sure it would be doing something outrageous, but I don't think he would've changed who he is. Even with the tragic cards he was dealt, a couple of years later and he's literally the same person he was before. It's been so long now, that I think we've all become used to this new way of life.

There's so many people in this world with similar situations but when you see it firsthand and up close it really affects you. We were invincible kids. Drinking and partying was just a part of life. Since the accident there have been a few times I got behind the wheel and stopped myself. Like I say when you see it up close it really puts life into perspective. Nowadays, we are past the traumatic stages but when you watch the day in the life of Kevin, I don't think there's anyone who can deal with today as well as him.

He's such a positive force, and beyond that he's a genuinely good person. He's the best person. He's my best friend.

5

Randy: Creature Double Feature

"I was supposed to be in the car with Kevin that night"

We grew up very wild. Our idea of a good time was getting your driver's license and getting a case of beer in the same night. We were proud of our rowdy reputation. So much that we nicknamed ourselves, "The Creatures." Our own club. Occupancy: Two bozos. Mission: To party. We knew it was stupid, but we were kids and we were dumb. I often wonder what would've happened if a guy like Kevin rolled into our school twenty years ago and how that would've changed us.

I was supposed to be in the car with Kevin that night. We grew up in the sticks and no one wanted to drive, so we preferred to just not drive and didn't care how drunk our friends were who were driving. We were just happy that they were willing to drive us around. Last minute before I was going to leave, I had grabbed my jacket, headed for the door and for whatever reason just changed my mind and decided to stay home. The next day I was at the beach with friends when we found out that Kevin was involved in an accident. Another guy who was there had mentioned it very nonchalantly and said he almost died. I wanted to jump over the railing and throttle him for saying it like that.

I left immediately and raced to the hospital. In the hospital the first person I saw was Kevin's dad, now we never got along, and he immediately hugged me and burst into tears. I've never had anyone close to me be in a situation like this and you don't know what to expect walking in. I'll never forget that moment I still have nightmares from it. Finding out your friend may die is an extremely difficult thing to come to terms with. And it really could've been any one of us. Kevin was already a shitty driver in my opinion so coupled with alcohol it was already a recipe for disaster but that's how we lived, just fast and wild. It's stupid to say but that's how we all lived it was just normal.

Our friendship was always ripping on one another, so it's hard to open up to your friends. Sometimes I wish his tongue got paralyzed so I didn't have to listen to his shitty jokes, but after he got into the accident, all I wanted to do was talk to him. But he wouldn't open up. Kevin never wanted to talk or see anybody bummed out over his condition; he really took it all upon himself. To this day I call him to go out and he says things like "Well, I can't really just roll out of bed because I'm uncomfortable." It's a real mind twist. You don't realize how much you take for granted.

I don't know what his dark days are like, but I know I could never do what he did and go through this. Seeing him in the hospital he was so positive and was more concerned for all of us. It was a real awakening. I can't tell you the years or months or days that we would go to see him, they all blend together. He was in the hospital for so long and I felt awful leaving him. I couldn't tell him anything that was going on in the outside world, whether it was about my life or life in general. But I still can't even put together what that was like for him. He was a prisoner in his own body. And it's something you can't anticipate happening. It just does. I guess that's why it's called an accident, but it never felt like reality.

One day at the hospital, the doctors told us he had about a 25% rate of survival, it's hard to put a number on that, like what do you do with it? That moment of uncertainty going home, I walked in the house, recounted the story and someone said, "I told you so." I remember thinking I am so incredibly pissed off. I

5

46

was ready to go to war. People were telling me that my friend deserved to die. And I was going through it. It was very real for me. Kevin is someone I talk to everyday and I've never told him about that.

After he came out of the hospital, he didn't want to be treated any differently but truthfully life was different. We still joke with him about the chair, and he just comes back with quips to beat us and make fun of himself more. There was a bit of a separation when he got out of the hospital as some of his friends dropped off and stopped coming around. There were a lot of fake pats on the back from people, but it just seems patronizing. His closest friends stuck with him. I remember his brother in law would even strap Kevin to his back like Chewbacca used to carry C-3PO in Star Wars and carry him onto the boat or up the stairs. I think he enjoys it now to some extent, the lazy prick that he is. I say that out of love. But I think he was taking the piss out of us at times. Basically, anything for a laugh. And that's the thing I love most.

Nowadays, I go to work very early in the morning and sometimes I call or text him at 5am just to ruin his day. But he's so positive you just can't antagonize him as much as you want to. But deep down you can tell he really is affected each day by this. The only thing he does really care for is his job. That's one thing I really can say with certainty and adoration. It isn't just a job; he legitimately is concerned for the kids he meets. When he tells us, he expects us to joke with him or make comment, but honestly, we all are so impressed with him. I've known him for over 30 years and he's the biggest dick I know, but I really love him. He's one of my favorite friends and I'm actually heading over to his place to see him tonight. It's 30 years later and I still look forward to seeing my friend every single time. I'm so happy he's still here and I really couldn't imagine a life without him. I love that kid, don't tell him that and please don't put that in the book.

6

*Kevin: The Speech Every Young
Person Should Hear*

*"These are real actions with real consequences and none of
which you ever want."*

I'm here to tell this story, and guys listen up, I think we are the ones who mostly make this mistake. We like to take risks, we don't always make the best choices, we like to push it a little bit… I was that guy. I was always pushing it I was always having fun and that's what led me to some poor choices. So anyway, I'm going to get right into it.

It was a big weekend; I have two sisters both younger. My sister Allison was graduating from high school that Friday. My little sister Hayley was younger, and Saturday was her ballet recital. I remember picking her up, catching her and twirling her around. I look back on that night and it never hit me that THAT night would be the last time I would ever do that. It never once dawned on me that that would be the night that changed life forever. I didn't think that way. And I never saw it coming. I'm sure that's why when a few hours later, the phone rang and it was a friend telling me about a house party I thought "Sweet, I'll be there." I grabbed a couple of beers and drank some before heading out. Now I'm gonna shoot straight with you here, this was pretty much the norm for me at this time.

When I got to the party I went inside and ran into my old buddies, mostly my hockey friends. I'm a Canadian, I'm from Vancouver, BC in case you haven't judged by now, but we love our hockey. And I grew up playing hockey. We had the "play hard party harder" mentality. And that party definitely carried on. That night we went from one party to another party to another, with me driving between each party that we went. This was of course, not a smart choice. My friends who had been riding with me all night started to notice the change that I didn't. I was stumbling out of the house, keys in hand, about to drive. They chipped in a few bucks and took a taxi and got that safe ride home. They have absolutely no regrets. Now for me looking back, I do. That cab was there. I could've got in. I also could've stayed at the party or I could've walked home. I could've called for a ride. My parents knew what I was up to, this wasn't a new thing. They always offered me that ride home if I needed it. Just call them.

My parents actually kept calling me that night. Calling and calling and calling. I just stopped answering. I wish I hadn't have. That ride was there. I'm not going to say that one day you won't be in a position like this because pretty much every one of you will. One day you may find yourself leaving a party, maybe as a driver, maybe as a passenger, maybe someone is offering you something you don't want to be around, maybe you just want out of a certain situation. Maybe there's someone you should call... Or maybe they're calling you. Remember these words, if you have that "out" and you have that ride home. Please recognize it and please, please take it. That's a sweet deal. Get home safe and while you're at it get your friends home safe. Looking back, I wish I had done just that. I had the opportunity, I could've called my dad and picked up my car the next day. I wouldn't be sitting in this wheelchair right now if I did. But I wanted to drive. I always drove.

It was a summer night with a little chill in the air. While I was warming the car up my buddy Brendon, an old hockey pal from growing up, tapped on the glass. He decided he's not taking the taxi anymore either. He hops in and away we go. My last memory of the night was an intersection. If I went right, I could've gone home. If I went left, I could party some more. And like so many nights before, we chose to go for the party. This was a crossroad of life. At the moment and we had no idea what lay ahead. All we were thinking about was what's more fun? What else can we get into? Let's party some more. We never made it to that party. I was driving way too fast, even if I was sober. But I did everything to excess. Excessively drunk, excessively speeding and I was a new driver, so I was inexperienced. The music was cranked loud, the beers were popped and in our hands. I was completely distracted. Any one of these things was enough on its own to cause a crash let alone, all of them going on at once.

Each little distraction increases your odds of an accident, until eventually it's a 100% chance. You too, will crash. Now let me be clear about the road and the conditions that night. This wasn't a sharp corner. There wasn't any ice present. An animal didn't jump out of nowhere. This was a road I was extremely familiar with. On any other day (if I was sober) I could've driven it with my eyes closed. It was a road I drove every single day. But that night it didn't matter. I didn't make the corner. The car shot straight ahead. The first thing it hit was a tiny little curb, but at the speed I was going it didn't matter. The faster you're going the harder you're going to crash. That tiny little curb launched my car into the air, and at that point I lost all control. It wasn't up to me anymore what happens. My decision was already made.

We hit the ground with a thunderous crash of metal and began rolling. It all happened in an instant. I don't know how many times it actually rolled over; it was a lot. But when it finally stopped it was upside down and a mangled mess of blood, metal and glass. Brendon and I were both critically hurt. He had hit his head. And it was serious. I hit my head as well but got lucky that mine was mild. My upper body was devastated though. The injuries sustained: dislocated left shoulder, separated right shoulder, busted both my collar bones, fractured vertebrae where my neck and back meet which did damage to my spine, I was torn to shreds from all the broken glass and completely covered in blood, on top of that I had a collapsed lung. It never occurred to me until years later how close I came to death that night until I met the paramedic from that night. Her name is Denise, I'll never forget her. She's the paramedic who bravely climbed out of the ambulance and into my car, saving my life. She's also a mom, and I met her years later when I spoke at her son's school. He was at my presentation and went home and told his mother about this story. As a lot of people do and I'm happy when they share the story, my only hope is that it helps someone else. But anyway, as he's telling his mom, he got to the part and told her my name, but she already knew. She knew the story; she was there that night and she'll never forget the horror that she saw. Being a parent herself to a boy, she saw a young man near death, helpless, battered and bloody, battling for his life. It's an image that you can't just wash away. She told me when we met up, that it's a miracle I'm alive.

The only reason at all besides pure luck, is that I wore my seatbelt. It didn't surprise me, because that is one thing that I never forget to do. I always wear my seatbelt. I don't even think about it, it's just a habit. And that one good driving habit and arguably the only good choice I made that night among so many bad ones... It's the only reason I'm here today. It saved my life.

If I hadn't worn the seat belt I could've been thrown from the car, it may have rolled over on me and crushed me killing me instantly. When it came to a stop, I was there hanging upside down. And as luck would have it, if I wasn't hanging upside down the blood and fluid would have pooled and collected in my lungs and I would've drowned. I was unconscious and there would have been nothing I could have done about it. I just never would have woken up from that night. I would be dead. But there I lay, unconscious as the fluid trickled out of me until we were found. I don't remember being found by the way. I didn't hear the first ambulance or the last. The crowd of police and rescue workers on scene all working together to get me out of the car, I don't remember any of it. Even as the Fire Department used the Jaws of Life, ripping away the metal door frame and tearing into my car to get me out... I would later learn it took over an hour just to free me from the vehicle. The ride to the hospital, the rush inside, all a blur to me. Doctors nurses, emergency personnel all working on saving my life... And I just don't remember any of it.

This next part has to do with my family and that dreaded phone call that no one ever wants to get. You think at times your family doesn't love you but let me get right to the point. They do. They love you a lot. More than you realize. That phone call is the worst moment of their life. To think my parents were asleep at home when the phone rang, instantly waking up and knowing that something must be wrong for the phone to ring so late at night. And those few words after a simple "Hello ... Mr. and Mrs. Brooks, your son has been in an accident." It's absolutely terrifying for a parent. However, there is one thing worse than the phone call. And that's the knock on the door. The knock on the door means – you didn't live. And well, there is no chance of "good news" or survival after death.

My family was lucky that night, they only got the phone call. They were told I may not make it to the morning, and they needed to rush to the hospital. They were also told to be prepared for what they were going to see, but there's no way to do that. To see a loved one so badly injured, wait... I wasn't injured, I was mangled, is a helpless feeling for anyone. Your loved one lying there in pain, dying, body falling apart, and you can look into their eyes and see the terror they feel and there isn't a single thing you can do to help them. It's heartbreaking to say the least. My body swelled up from the trauma, it looked like one big bruise, my lip was split right through and dangling from my face, my arm was torn to shreds from going through the window and rolling around in the glass. The doctors even thought they may have to amputate, it looked that bad. And I'm so glad that didn't happen. I can't imagine losing an arm AND being in a wheelchair. What do you do with one arm and a wheelchair? A lot of circles my friend, ONLY circles. That's right, I have wheelchair jokes, they're not good ones but you'll hear a few more as the story continues. I like comedy. It really helps. I actually started doing comedy about three years ago. And in those three years I have done a lot of comedy all over North America. I still haven't done any stand up, I like to call it "I can't stand up comedy." Sometime when the tears dry up, all that is left to do is crack jokes and try to bring light to the darkness and pain.

So that night I really could have lost more than I did, and I am forever grateful that I didn't.

There I was in this hospital room, tubes stuck in me, machines buzzing and beeping all around, doctors prodding and checking on me all the while surrounded by my family that was just praying that I would live. My eyes were open in a blank stare, absolutely no one home. The doctors told my family that it was a twenty MAYBE thirty percent chance that I would even live. My younger sister, Allison, rushed into the room and was immediately escorted out, she couldn't see me like this. In the hours that passed I was moved to another hospital where I continued fighting for my life. But I also started fighting the doctors and nurses. Apparently, the morphine and painkillers they put me on to help ease the pain were giving me hallucinations and creating fantastic scenarios in my head. I would see them chatting to one another and saying things like "When his parents leave tonight let's unplug him from the breather, so he dies." But this was all in my head. It was my mind playing out a nightmare into my reality. I was so sure that it was real. But it wasn't. None of it was.

The other issue was that I didn't have a voice. I literally could not form words. So, I couldn't even explain to them what I THOUGHT was happening. There was a breather in my throat that cut off my vocal cords and completely shut them off. And that's probably why I started swinging and getting so violent with the people who were just trying to save me. I was terrified, and I couldn't say anything about it even if I tried. I felt for the first time, completely helpless. I started flailing around and yanking tubes out, I was a menace to the people who were just trying to help me. But I just didn't realize that. At that point they strapped me down to the bed. I felt crazy. There was nothing I could do. I didn't just have a tube in my throat either. There were six more down my rib cage for the collapsed lung, two more up my nostrils, down my throat and to my stomach. One was pumping nutrients in while the other pumped stomach infection out. The worst tube of all though was the size of your pinkie finger and for the fellas reading this, I'm sure you can guess where the worst tube of all was inserted. Yea, that's right. It went in there. It's extremely uncomfortable and incredibly sensitive. You may be crossing your legs at this point; I know I would be if I could (another wheelchair joke). Anyway, just trust me I didn't want that catheter either. So, that was my summer. And it all started with a party.

And as I came off the medication, I became more aware of my surroundings but still had no idea what had happened yet. They were afraid if they told me what happened that I may give up and quit fighting so hard for my own survival. Until one day, I started to ask questions. I still couldn't speak, but you know how moms are. My mom she took the whole summer off work so she could sit with me and learn how to read lips. It's the only way we could communicate. But it felt good, I could finally tell someone what was going on in my head and ask the questions that have been rolling around in there. If you think refraining from talking isn't very hard, try it for a day or even an hour. Don't answer the phone, go for fast food and try to communicate even what you want to drink or ask where the bathroom is, all without speaking. See how incredibly frustrating something we so easily take for granted can be. And this was my life. So, as my mother spent more time with me and explained that she could now communicate and read my lips I decided to ask her the one big question that really has been bothering me. That question was... "Why can't I move my legs?" I had no clue. And there was my mom, about to break the news to me. The news that had broken her heart, and would break it a million times more telling her first born, her only son, Kevin, you're paralyzed. News that her son, the athlete, the active guy, her healthy baby boy will never walk again. As the words came out of her mouth, "Kevin, I'm really sorry... you're paralyzed." Now I know even as you read this book, you may have seen me speak or even noticed a picture perhaps on the book cover, so it's no secret that I'm in a wheelchair. But you have to remember my life wasn't always like this. I was just like you.

Sitting on the couch watching television, you can pop up and walk to the fridge, grab a soda, even grab those chips from the top shelf, (I was 6 foot tall before the accident and now I'm hovering around 4 feet). The most basic of life tasks are now forever altered. And I wasn't ready for that, no one can be. I was young, healthy active, just living life and loving every bit of it. Looking forward to the future, making plans, for things I wanna do, things I wanna try, adventures I want to go on. And then suddenly it stops. Those plans will never happen. It's not your life anymore. For me, it was I'm never going to skateboard again, never snowboard again, never stage dive a concert again, never run down the beach and feel the water on my toes, play frisbee, football, wakeboard, the list goes on and on and on. And that's my list and I'm sure sitting there you have your own list of things that you love and love doing. Now imagine one day you wake up and that list is gone. It's all gone. Now what? I look back to that day and my mom told me "Kevin, you can't move your legs." I tried so hard to force them; they wouldn't budge. I started to panic. I tried harder and harder but still nothing, not even an inch. So, I stopped and figured I'd try something a little simpler, and I thought maybe I can just wiggle my toes. That's easy enough.

After an accident, it's one of the questions they ask you. "Can you wiggle your toes." I know it seems ridiculous but it's true. You may have just done it now as you're reading this... Easy huh? So simple. I wanted you to do that. And now I'm making you aware of it, so you're trying to make yourself not do it again... Whoops there it is. You just did it. I gotcha. And even if you didn't because you're being stubborn it's ok, because I know you will eventually. I hope you always can. That's something I wish for all of you reading this. Anyway, the point is it's something so simple and well, I haven't done it in well over a decade. The closest I get is to a leg spasm every now and then. That's always fun to freak out your friends. "Guys it's a miracle I can walk! No... No, I can't." I laugh. They don't. Much like most of my jokes, but hey at least someone is laughing.

Back in the hospital room, my mom was sitting there tears in her eyes, delivering news that she's been dreading. Her heart is broken. And I don't know how to deal with the news she just told me. I don't want to believe it. We both start crying. And then I asked what happened. She told me I was in a car crash. I still didn't remember. But I can't say that I was surprised to hear that either. Not from the way I lived my life, it felt like par for the course. And like I said about distractions, you play with them enough times and you will have 100% chance of getting into an accident. And I didn't drive any differently than I had a dozen times before. No different than how my buddies drove and no different than how you may have even driven before. I think we all have done it at one point or another. Do you ever remember a night where you woke up the next day and had a sigh of relief thinking "Whew, how did I make it home last night?" I'm the exception that didn't make it home. And it can happen to you as well is what I want you to remember. There's nothing more special about you or me or anybody, it can just happen. Any time.

I'm not going to try and point fingers, but teenagers are way overrepresented in car crashes. And it's mostly the guys (sorry dudes) But, it's true. We get into a car and we always wanna "See what it can do." Or our ego says we can drive when clearly, we can't. We wanna drive fast, we wanna show off to our buddies, and after a few beers its ok, I'm fine to drive home. But we aren't. Taking those risks is unnecessary. And even being on your phone, or just being fatigued just any kind of distraction is a risk. Have you not been in a vehicle whether as a driver or passenger where one of those risks were going on? Maybe more than one? It happens. For me and my friends this was pretty much any time I hopped into a vehicle. But it wasn't just in vehicles that we made bad choices. We were the rowdies we were the partiers of the school. I was nicknamed the "Creature" in high school. Yea, figure that one out. I wasn't staying home on weekends to get that nickname.

On our skateboards were crashes, slams and there were bails but we never got really hurt. We always made it home in one piece. And I think it's for that reason that we started to feel like we were invincible as most teenagers do. We were way too cocky for our own good. It wasn't a skill that we had; it was purely just luck. And every time we went out, we rolled those dice. And one thing I can tell you for certain, is that luck does NOT last forever. Especially if you mess with it. Don't tempt fate with your actions. You can push your luck, push it, push it, push it, and then what happens is one night your luck runs out. And there's no turning back from that point forward. I learned that the hard way. I'm paralyzed. There's no cure for that.

There I was lying in a hospital bed and all those thoughts came crashing down on me all at once. And it really felt like my life had come to an end. My attitude has changed since, but that was my initial reaction and how I felt. I just needed some good news. Something good to lift me up, even if just a little bit. Let my friends be ok, at least they made it out of that night and I'm the only one who's punished. I must've had some buddies with me, I didn't remember who, but I knew I never partied alone. So, I started guessing friends' names, and each time I guessed my mom would shake her head "No." And then I ran out of names. I had an overwhelming sigh of relief. Thankfully, none of my buddies were with me that night. Everyone is ok. I didn't do what I did to my-self to anyone else. I can live with that. And then I hear my buddy Brendon was with me... At first my thoughts were just random. That's rad I thought. I hadn't seen Brendon in a while, we hadn't played hockey together in probably 8 years at this point.

Last I saw Bren was at another party months before and before that a lot when he was dating my sister Allison. I was never that over-protective weirdo brother. Don't date my sister. Brendon was a good dude. He treated Allison well. They were happy. Then they split up as most high school couples eventu-ally do. I remember things being a bit awkward at first when that happened between Brendon and I and looking back now with a clearer memory of the early parts of that night I remember that we were having fun, letting the past be the past. Sadly, I also think this may have been why he hopped in with me at the end of the night. He wanted to be bro's. I was down for that too. But that wasn't to be the case for much longer. As I laid there with my mom I began to wonder, "How's Bren doing and what he's up to?" So, I ask my mom.... My mom stopped and said "Kev, ... Brendon died, Brendon's dead and I'm really sorry." It's not easy to say. And it's not easy to hear, or even type on this page. I don't know what was in your mind when you woke up this morning before you lifted this book and opened it up but as I sit here, all I can think right now in this moment is "I'm about to tell a stranger, countless strangers that I killed my buddy."

My friend died in my car, under my care. And it's because I drove fast, I drove distracted, I drove impaired. I was reckless and took risks I didn't need to take. Nothing can prepare a person for that news. I can tell you; I didn't want to believe it. I still don't want to believe it, but it happened. The last thing he did was hop in my car, and then my mom told me he was gone. Gone and buried. She mentioned his funeral and that's when it hit me hard. I couldn't take it back. I thought maybe he was in the other room getting repaired, Brendon's a tough guy, he's an athlete he can get better just like I was. I didn't know how much time had passed. But she told me this happened a month ago while I was in a coma. He was cremated. They aren't saving him, and he is never coming back. And at that moment, all my actions and the consequences got very real. And then it dawned on me, Brendon's family. His mother his father, brothers, sisters, friends everyone we grew up with and his family playing with mine at the ice rink. What have I done to these people's lives? And I don't know a word or series of words that I can share with you right now to describe the feeling. But it's a feeling that I don't wish upon anyone. And that's the reason I'm writing these words now. So, I can share it with you and in doing so I hope, and I beg that you NEVER go through what I did. So much could have been avoided that night. And I don't need to know you to not wish this upon you.

I asked my mom how Brendon's family was doing. She told me they were struggling to get through each day. They lost their son, their brother and so much more. She also told me his parents were calling the house. That was something I was very surprised to hear. They were calling for updates on me. They wanted to know how I was doing. To give you an idea of who his parents are and the love they have, at Brendon's funeral I heard they even stopped it and asked everyone to pray for me because at the time I was still clinging to life. They even started a charity fund to chip in for me to help with my recovery once they found out I was paralyzed. Can you imagine? At their son's funeral. When I first heard this, I immediately reversed the role and thought what if that had happened to me? What if my sister got into a crash from someone else's careless actions? Would I be out there praying for them? Would I be raising money for them or caring about their well-being?... I don't think so. They could've so easily hated me.

And no one would ever think twice about that. But they didn't. And this is something I think about every day of my life. It's a true testament to who they are. I don't think I would be writing these words or maybe even here today without the support they showed me.

As I laid in the bed, I know I'm supposed to have hope and want to get better and get through this, but not then. It was the worst day of my life. And I didn't want to get better. I didn't think I deserved to at all. I started asking other questions like "Why did I live?" or "Why did Brendon have to die?" "Why am I here". And mostly "Do I deserve to be alive?" and every time the same answer came back to me in my head. The answer was "No." I don't deserve to be alive. Not after what I've done. I'm not strapped down to the bed anymore. Now I can do something about it. My plan was as soon as everyone leaves I'll yank my breather out, it won't be that difficult. It won't take even that long for me to kill myself. Just end it. Easy. I'm out, see ya. Gone. But every time I reached for the tube; I heard a voice in my head saying "Don't do it.... I wanna live, I wanna live I wanna live." So, I didn't. I made a choice that day, and I'm still here because of that choice. And I'm not gonna say it's not an easy road by any means. But I do not regret that choice. Not at all.

And it was a long road. Things I could never imagine. I had to learn and re-learn. Things I could never fathom having to learn or do in new, restrictive ways. I had to learn to breathe on my own without the help of a machine. Which was terrifying because I was so weak. It was a struggle just to fight for air and try to take a breath and strengthen a collapsed lung. Going to the bathroom suddenly involved tubes and bags. Pills, constant medication, nurses coming in and having to change my clothes for me. That wasn't very fun at all. It's very tough to keep it together and look cool after you just pooped your pants as an adult. I learned that the hard way. Just to eat, I remember they dyed water and canned pears blue because it had been so long since I had eaten that they were afraid that I may have forgotten how and swallowed water into my lungs. You don't want food in your lungs. So, after I finished eating, they would take another apparatus and suction it out of my lungs like a giant vacuum cleaner to make sure no blue dye of food or water had gone into my lungs. Just the smallest little things. It took about two months for me to learn these things again. Also, I was still in the hospital which always makes you feel uncomfortable. They call it "white coat syndrome" when you have increased anxiety being around doctors and others in white coats. It's a real feeling. I just wanted to go home, and I couldn't. There was a whole other list of things I would need to learn to do before that could ever happen. I was going to be sent to a rehab center first.

In rehab I had to learn to use the wheelchair of course. But mostly it's just the day to day stuff, that you know how to do but you wouldn't know how to do stuck seated in a chair. For example, in the morning, you wake up you jump out of bed you hop to the shower. You dry off and get dressed. Now, next time you really want a challenge, just try to put on a pair of pants sitting down. Don't use your legs or your hips. You can only use your arms. I'm actually paralyzed from the chest down, so I don't have any use of my ab muscles and it's your core that keeps you stable. I'm telling you, just try it. See how long it takes you. How do you get those pants on? Don't even get me started on skinny jeans. Woof, whatta nightmare. Thank God those are going out of fashion now, eh? I still have a few pairs though. Now I only bust them out for special occasions like heavy metal shows and just hope it doesn't rain.

Just to roll over in bed took hours of therapy for weeks at a time. Think about that. How simple it is. But without core mobility how do you roll over. What you actually do is you rock your top half back and forth until you can throw one arm over and push yourself up. The first time I ever got halfway over I was so excited. It was like the first kickflip I ever did on a skateboard.

Now, it took me a few more months to learn how to even sit up from a laying down position. I would have to just push and pull myself up using only my arms. I tend to also have to fight spasms that stiffen everything up. Just atrophied muscles from not doing anything at all. It made it extremely difficult.

After about four months of this rehab I was able to take my first solo shower and dress myself. I was so stoked. I had to call all my friends and tell them. Guys, can you imagine calling up your boys and being like, "Hey man guess what?! I just showered and dressed myself today... It only took me two and a half hours." I'm sure that was the most random phone call they ever got but they all remained supportive and would cheer me on, telling me to "Keep it up, you'll be home soon." And it's that support from friends and family that's so important. To know it's there, and no one knew what to say. I think we always struggle to find the right words, but no one ever really knows them. Just be there. Be the person you have always been to that person. It meant a lot to just have my buddies in the hospital treating me as they always did. I needed those laughs. Remember, it's not what you say to people it's just about being there for them. It's just about showing up.

One of my buddies brought me a pair of ear buds so I could listen to music. I haven't listened to any in very long time. I'm a huge punk rock fan, and I remember putting them in my ears and just turning the volume all the way up. NOFX, one of my favorite bands. I could finally listen to music instead of the sounds of the hospital. I would drown it all out with the ripping guitar and screaming vocals of my favorite band. And I'd listen to them over and over until the batteries died. They were small glimmers of light in a very dark and difficult time. Behind those victories I was able to still smile. But behind those smiles there was still pain, fear, uncertainty and mostly guilt. I would think to myself; I feel happy and how could I feel happy right now in this moment knowing my friend and passenger, Brendon is dead? I thought about that a lot then and I still do. I think about his family and how their son and their brother isn't coming home. I think about their weddings and family celebrations around the holidays and how he isn't there. And how difficult it must be. I'm smiling because I got into some denim today and how are they feeling today? At this point I haven't seen them; I haven't spoken to them.

One day my mom handed me a piece of paper with Brendon's parents' phone number on it and it was the most difficult phone call I ever made. I remember picking up the phone and putting it down, fighting back the tears what do I even say? We spoke for a while and we both cried, but through the tears I was invited to their family home. It took a while before I could get a day pass to even leave the rehab center, and it took a number of different people just to lift me into the passenger seat of the car and get me there. But, off we went to Brendon's family's house. After we arrived there were stairs to get in, but Brendon's father grabbed the back of my chair and my mom grabbed the front and they bumped me up the stairs backwards. Bump. Bump. Bump. Up the stairs and into the house. We were in the living room and his parents were trying to keep it light, and I was listening. I also remember looking around at all the pictures. All the pictures on the mantle, in the hallways, and on the side tables. You know the types of photos I'm talking about. Your parents probably have the same ones of you in their homes too. If you have brothers or sisters, those family photos and group portraits, teen photos, school photos, graduation pictures, everything from your baby life to young adult life your parents have them all. And there they were in front of me. I was looking at all of them all at once. And it was then, that I fell apart. Because I know one person in those pictures is never coming home again. And I'm the sole reason as to why. Why that person will never take another photo with his family. His father led me outside and said something to me that I could never have expected. And I didn't know what to say next. He said they weren't out to get me, hate me or attack me. The way they chose to see it was that night both Brendon and I made that poor decision ourselves. And we both knew better. He knew better than to hop in my car that night and I knew better that I shouldn't be driving. We all know better not to get in a car in these situations. And if you didn't know before and you need a reminder just open this book or just wiggle your toes because these are real actions with real consequences.

So, I hope you're taking it all in and getting it today. Brendon's parents just like mine always offered that "ride home" too. His dad said "You both had it you both chose not to take it and you both could've used it because you both like to party and drive fast. If it was any other night our son could've been driving, and you could've been the passenger. Brendon could be the one in the chair and you could be gone forever, and we would be talking to your family. We can't put it all on you. It took both of you." I never thought about that. It could've been the very next weekend and very different circumstances should I have been the passenger. And I was shocked his father said that me. A grieving man, so upset with his son's loss was able to forgive me for taking that from him and I still don't know how they can do it. Sometimes I still wonder to this day, and I've asked him on multiple occasions how he can do it. And the answer has always been the same. And that answer is "It's easier to forgive me than it is to hate me. Anger, resentment and revenge hold no place in my life." Brendon's family taught me a great deal about forgiveness and it's something I hold dear and always will. And speaking of forgiveness the journey of self-forgiveness that I am on also began that day and it will last my lifetime.

Brendon's family would extend their forgiveness again about a year and a half later when I rolled in front of a judge pleading guilty to the charges from the crash. Dangerous driving causing death. Impaired driving causing death. These are very serious charges. And even 20 years ago in Canada where sentences tend to be more lenient than the USA, there was still a very good chance I could be going to prison. I was ok with that though. I was brought up to be accountable and face the consequences of my choices and actions. I am sure to say that the only reason I did not do time was because I had a lenient, empathetic judge who looked at me, a young man, sitting in a wheelchair at the prime of my life wearing the death of my friend on my shoulders and flat out said that "The life sentence I imposed on myself was far worse than any sentence behind bars." He also informed me that when the courts reached out to Brendon's family for a victim impact statement that they not only showed forgiveness and support but that they totally went to bat for me. They kept me out of jail. They gave me a second chance, and this is what I am doing with it.

Looking back, I will never forget going to Brendon's family's house, seeing his parents, sitting with them in Brendon's living room and having those conversations with them. That man to man, that heart to heart conversation with his dad out on the back patio all the while with how cool they were being to me, was the hardest thing I've ever done in my life. The hardest. And it's a visit I don't wish upon anyone. I don't know, maybe keep that visit in mind when you're out and about. When you're driving around with your friends because it's not the driver who tends to get the worst of it. It's the passengers. It's the people who chose to ride in your car. The people who chose to trust you with their safety that wind up getting the most hurt. So, just realize it's not worth it to make these poor choices and take these risks and then live with that for the rest of your life. It's not easy. It's quite the opposite. And I am not trying to be a party pooper here or a bummer. I am a dude with a mullet, hand tattoos and a wheelchair covered in punk rock stickers. I have fun. I live life. As we all should. So of course, have fun, live your life, be young, but just don't cross that line. It's all a choice. We can choose to either be the friend that puts our friends in harm's way or the one who safeguards them and keeps them out of harm's way. It's up to you. To really be a friend, you want to be the one who looks out for your buddies. Who protects them. Which do you want to be? If you can't easily make that decision then flip flop the situation and ask yourself, are you ready to be liable for those consequences? Are you ready to face that friends' family? The weight on your conscience every day... Is it REALLY worth that risk?

I left Brendon's family's' house and left with their support and it meant the world to me and it still does. It was also a taste of home. I hadn't been home in months, and I really wanted to get back to my own home. My goal was to get home before Christmas and that was pretty ambitious you know? My friends and family kept coming by the hospital and tried to keep my spirits up, which was nice, but one person started showing up less and less... My girlfriend, Robyn. And it hurt. Robyn and I met in high school; we were both each other's first loves. We were both outdoorsy active people, especially snowboarding but mostly just anything outside. She rode a horse, I rode a skateboard, we taught each other a few tricks on either. She was an honor roll student, all straight A's looking to be a veterinarian, and now IS a veterinarian, but in high school she was dating a guy nicknamed "The Creature" as I told you was my moniker. From the outside we didn't look like a perfect match, but boy, did we love each other. We came from different lifestyles, we had different priorities. She was not a fan of parties, she was not a fan of the way I drove my car, I knew that we talked about it many times. And it wasn't just my girlfriend. My family and my friends had those same concerns for me. There have been a lot of those talks. I'm sure you can relate; I think we all have had a "talking to" at one point or another. We all get it. But it's up to us as individuals whether or not we listen. My problem is I chose not to listen when I should have. And I can't put into words how grateful I am to this day for all of my friends and family who stood by me when I needed them the most, but Robyn, she was done. And in hindsight I really can't blame her because that wasn't the healthiest relationship for her. But at first, man did it hurt. Adding a broken heart to everything else going on was my breaking point. We all have one. That was mine. I just gave up. I lost it. I lost hope. I felt like everything was gone. Of course, it wasn't. I still had family and friends and things to live for and fight for. But at that time, I was done fighting. I couldn't find anything positive to grab hold of. I put a negative spin on everything. I couldn't go out with my friends and try to cheer myself up. I was stuck in a hospital room unable to move, I was trapped with my thoughts. I didn't want to be around. Then the depression sunk in.

I learned a few things about depression. It creeps up on you when you're at your lowest and most vulnerable. It's very empty, it comes on and crushes your spirit all at once. Depression says things to you like "No one is here, no one cares about you, there's nothing left to live for, you have nothing left to give." Hearing all those thoughts were scary. At that point I became suicidal. I would think about death every day, but the irony is that I wasn't even out of the hospital bed at that point. I couldn't kill myself even if I wanted to. And that's where I needed to be. I was being monitored. I started talking to a counselor. The counselor would visit me every day, and I didn't want to talk to a counselor, I didn't want to talk to anybody. But it's not like I could run away. And it proved healthy to talk to someone. Somebody who wasn't in the immediate situation. Somebody who had some advice about what was going on. And it wasn't like it was even things I couldn't wrap my head around. He told me to keep writing. I was writing a lot at the time, and they told me to keep doing that and get my thoughts out and down on the page. I would write anything and everything. I would write rants, I would write rhymes, I would write letters to the girl who broke my heart. It was a letter that I would never send. But I wrote them anyway. I was told to keep writing and that it was supposed to be a positive outlet. And it did help, and it taught me how important it is to have positive outlets in our lives.

Years later now, I have a hand cycle. It allows me to get outside and breathe fresh air and exercise. Such a great way to feel better about myself on a bad day. I love cooking and have been cooking vegan for the last four years trying to live a healthy, cruelty free lifestyle. I also have a guitar that I learned to play. A few lessons from a metalhead who arrived at my home decked out in Toronto Maple Leaf socks, Metallica shirt and a bandana that coupled with some time on the internet and I was solid. Boom, now, I am playing and singing songs. Such a great way to express any emotion or pass the time on cold and rainy days. I do comedy in the evening. It's a blast. It's a bit dark. A bit demented, but hey, I was demented long before I was ever an inspiration. Humor is so important. Making light of those things that we cannot control or change. Making others laugh, bringing joy. Which leads to me to my absolute favorite thing of all which is doing the presentations in schools. Speaking to kids who were my age which is a difficult age and time in life to navigate, even at the best of times. I meet so many young people who are struggling. Everyone has a story. I know there are people in the room at every talk I give, people who are reading these words right now who are struggling. Struggling with loss, or heartbreak or health issues. Struggling with mental illness, addiction and self-harm. Young people who may have a suicide note hidden away in their bedroom at home who are waiting for that moment to end it all. Thinking life will never get better. And I am here to tell you, it does get better. No matter how bad it gets, it can and will always get better. Maybe not on a timetable that you wish for, but if you can force yourself to find little joys each day, those little joys become habit and when you add them all up you become a happier person. Mood really is a habit. This accident was the worst thing that ever happened to me and those around me, but it afforded me the ability to turn it into something so much more positive for more people than you can imagine. And I learned that being able to turn those negative, terrible moments in our lives into something positive is the greatest healer of all.

Also, I have learned that it is important to talk about the things in our lives with others. Maybe not to entire room full of strangers like I do, but talk to somebody. If we speak about whatever it is that is troubling us, then we are dealing with it. Every time I grab a microphone and share this story I am working through things. I am getting it out. It's cathartic. It's a release. It's almost like the students I speak to have become my counselors. I know they didn't sign up for that, but I offer to be that person who will hear them out in return. So many young people write me. Some of the messages are a quick short and sweet thank you. I needed that. Some are pages and pages of words neatly organized and checked for grammar. Some messages are total rants that bounce all over the place. But I read every word and every message because I know that it took a lot to reach out and be vulnerable and to let that guard down. I know that those messages are often times a cry for help. And I write every person back because everyone deserves to know that there is someone out there who has their back. Someone out there who cares. Nobody is taking this world on alone.

We all need a little reminder from time to time that life is a gift. That the little things are worth celebrating. That the difference between a bad day and a good day can just be a change of attitude and perspective. Just one night. Tomorrow is always a new day. It's a fresh start if we allow it to be and let go of what was hurting us and holding us down yesterday. It takes effort. For sure it does. But having that peace and happiness in life is worth the effort. If I can do it, anyone can do it. I realized that attitude is such a huge factor in how we receive the day and how the day receives us. My attitude changed when I was at my lowest point in GF Strong not wanting to face rehab or paralysis. Or my broken heart or the fact that my friend was dead. One thing I will always remember that really helped me change my perspective on things was a talk I had with my physiotherapist Cindy. Cindy and I got a long great. She was a very spiritual person. She was going on self-finding retreats and doing yoga way back when before these things were trendy and cool. And in the daytime, she worked at rehabilitation center trying to teach people who had recently faced life altering injuries how to physically adapt to the changes in their bodies. How to live in many respects. I was feeling sorry for myself a bit. I didn't want to learn how to be in a wheelchair. I wanted to walk. Why put all this time into learning to be in a wheelchair? That was the last thing I wanted. How does a person work for something, work harder than they ever have worked, for something they don't even want? Not even in the very least bit. I often addressed these situations with sarcasm and cracking smartass jokes. And credit to Cindy, she would laugh. She humored me. But she also saw past the façade. Beyond the macho badass I was trying to portray. The only way my confused mind then, knew how combat the turmoil and struggle that I was dealing with every moment of every day. One day we were in the rehab gym and she was trying to teach me to transfer from the rehab bed into my wheelchair. Something that might sound easy but with no core, thrashed shoulders and a lot of dead weight to throw and balance was seemingly impossible. I didn't want to learn. I didn't want to try. Cindy said "Hey I know that you are struggling with all of this and I get it. Who wouldn't be? I also understand that you want to walk again. Who wouldn't? But you never know if that will happen again or when it might. Never, ever lose hope. But also, in the meantime, you need to learn these things so that you can make the most of today." Basically, figure out how to make the best of today and never stop hoping for something bigger and better tomorrow. Those simple words have stuck with me to this day. I wake up every day and do what I can to make it a good day. A great day. An amazing day. Sometimes I succeed. Sometimes I fail miserably. But hey, I have tomorrow to look forward to. Tomorrow and a fresh start is just a sleep away.

So, I put that effort. In each day trying to heal and get home for Christmas as I told you, and I did it. I made it home a few days before Christmas and had a rude awakening. I forgot my dad's house was all stairs. So, I moved into a little apartment with my mom. And my brain had to adapt, I had to figure things out. Wheelchair access became every thought everywhere I went. It's all I would think about. But I started to figure things out, I figured "If we don't give up, we start to find a way and there is a way." And yea, it's not going to be the old way. In fact, 99.999% of the time it wasn't going to be the old way. It was going to be the new way. Because it had to be. So, I started to learn the new way. Which was hard, but it led me back to my favorite spots. Like the skateboard park, look, I still have four wheels. I went up to the mountain and tried "sit skiing", that was pretty cool. I never thought I'd be back up on the mountain again. The only one I was missing now was the beach. That one is a little tricky, if you've ever tried sand and wheels it's not so easy. But we found a lake near home with a pathway down to the edge of the sand. I was happy with that and have the view of the beach. And it was close by. The lake wasn't exactly the ocean, but it was a close second. I didn't realize how far away I was from it though until I saw my sister Hayley splashing around in it. So, there I am, I'm watching my sister, this little kid who I love so much, and I want nothing more to be splashing around with her in that lake... And that hit me hard. Cuz I realized things will be different from now on. Things are different. From now on, I'll be sitting over here while she's in the water. I can only watch her from a distance, doing the things we used to do together. And it hit me that that's what I get. I took away someone else's big brother and future uncle. If he can't play with his kid sister anymore why should I? I also thought what did my sister, Hayley do to deserve this though? I thought about that. She just misses playing with her big brother.

I remember it was her birthday and when the cake and candles would come out, mom or dad would tell Hayley to make a wish, and she never said a word. She'd just look at me. Her big brother. With a hopeful look in her eyes, and I knew what she was wishing for, but it was never going to come true. And I can't give it to her. So, I sat on the edge of the sand and figured there's gotta be a way to do this. I figured out if you lean back and do a wheelie and keep those front wheels out of the sand it would stop getting stuck. It wasn't easy to do, and it took a lot of force on my arms to push myself through the sand. But I made it to the lake. And I splashed my little sister. And it was a big brother little sister moment that I'll never forget. I also remember feeling that there was something special about this lake. Something that drew me back there over and over again. I didn't know how or why or what, but I just had to.

Not long after, I met a man named Rick Hansen, and he's from Vancouver where I live as well. Rick actually rolled a wheelchair around the circumference of the world as a paraplegic to raise awareness. Now he has a huge foundation, and they invited me to join them and do a fundraiser. I said "Yes." Now it was time for me to start doing some good. It wasn't a one-man mission by any means. We had family, we had friends, we had the community, volunteers, a lady named Joyce who did water therapy out of her home and offered her pool to train for others to swim for free. I went to skateboard shops, and restaurants and the gym I attended and asked for donations. Everything, you name it. Six months later I returned to that lake and I swam across it. In doing so I raised a ton of money for charity and what an amazing feeling that was. I'd never done anything like that before. And now I was hooked. I was hooked on that feeling and I wanted more of it. Not long after that I was invited to speak at a school. I was terrified. I didn't know anything about public speaking. I was more afraid of public speaking than I was about swimming paralyzed across a lake. But if I did that, I could definitely just "talk" to people. Then one after another I got asked to return and speak at more schools. I never did think I'd go past the area code that I lived in. And here I am today, I've been all across North America and spoke to over 500,000 kids in schools. Eight provinces across Canada and thirty states across America and counting. And I'm so grateful to be here. And I have no intentions of slowing down anytime soon.

As long as I can get this many young people into a room, and it makes a difference in people's lives then I'll keep doing this. It's also the reason I wrote this book. I want kids and teens to have a readily available version, so if you ever feel down or depressed and need a little hope you can pick it up and read a few pages and be reminded that it's not over. As bad as it gets, nothing has to be over. It's tough to lose friends or family to needless accidents, so I'm here and I'm going to keep doing this for all of you. Along my journey, Brendon wasn't the only friend of mine to lose his life too soon.

I had a friend named Jordan, he killed himself. I actually got the news while I was in front of an entire school. I was just about to be introduced and begin my presentation when my phone went off. I answered and found out. Definitely the hardest presentation I ever had to do. I was balling my eyes out throughout the whole speech and I couldn't help it. And with that I brought up his story to everyone, I felt I had to explain what was going on. I needed to tell his story as well. And I wanted to honor my friend, but man did it hurt just to say his name. And with that another mission was born. I began to speak to kids about the dangers of depression and suicide prevention. I lost another friend, Chris. Chris was shot to death. He was just in the wrong place at the wrong time. Just a random act of violence. And I had a presentation that day too! A lot of tears, but again I felt, man, this is gonna hit people. A lot of folks have lost people to violence, to guns, to unnecessary crimes. Again, these are all preventable. All of these things. It's not fair that their family this year celebrates Christmas without them. It never had to be that way. And just when I thought I was through losing buddies, my inbox lit up again. This time it was yet another friend, also named Chris. Chris was a skateboarder like me. When I was in the hospital, he tagged the skateboard ramps in Cloverdale with graffiti saying, "Get Well Soon Kevin", just to show me I was never forgotten. Chris liked to smoke weed, it's not my thing but I get it. Whatever, I'm not here to judge anyone. Last thing we know is his wife is putting their twins to bed. Chris goes to have a smoke before bed and watch some TV. Nothing new. But he never makes it to bed. His wife eventually finds him. On the couch, slouched over not breathing. She tries to resuscitate him. No response. By the time emergency personnel arrive Chris is dead. I'm not sure that anyone knows whether there was fentanyl in the weed he smoked or if it was intentionally put in there. But this drug is so strong that even a miniscule amount from something as simple as cross contamination from a dealer using the same table or scale for both substances is enough to kill a person. It's scary and it is so sad.

Fentanyl and opioids in general have become an epidemic and it is scary. People think it is safe to take pain killers because a doctor prescribed them or because they come from a pharmacy or drug store and they are technically a legal substance. But they are highly addictive, and their misuse is taking thousands of lives away every single year. Then the pills run out. People resort to street drugs like heroin which are cheaper and sometimes easier to get. But who knows what a person is getting when purchasing street drugs from some sketchy source or even a reliable source if there is such a thing? Fentanyl is turning up in every kind of drug because it is cheap, and its high potency. It's almost 100 times stronger than heroin and it is absolutely deadly. There is no high out there worth that. I just want to be clear.

The day that Chris died I had a presentation to give that morning. And a lot of tears at that one too, another one of my buddies gone forever. Another story, and hopefully another lesson for all of you. It sucks losing friends. Losing one friend is too many. Four friends... That is way too many. Whenever I do a presentation, I have four empty chairs on the stage and a lot of folks think it's for a question and answer session later. It's not. It's for my friends. Those four friends sitting beside me. Those four who were gone too soon, and I'm the fifth. The one who escaped death. They're always with me and I will always think about them. Brendon, Jordan, Chris and Chris. I love to think they're sitting beside me in spirit and sharing their story as I've shared mine. I'm hoping now at this point that you're hearing the story, that you're feeling it, use it, share it and Just wiggle your toes to be reminded of it should you ever forget and need a little boost. Please. Because from this day forward, this story is ours, it doesn't become a story of yours or your friends' or your families'. This is why we are here. This is why I'm writing this. A voice to share the story. I wonder sometimes if that's why I survived. To share the story. To save others from this pain. To inspire others to make wiser choices in their day-to-day life.

Now at this point, I have found this journey of life, this struggle, it's just good to talk about it. Reach out and talk to someone, anyone really. Reach out for support to those you care about, believe me they care about you too. I really love that I get to meet a lot of people all over the world. I'm meeting people everyday. And a lot of those young people have reached out to me and they shared their stories with me as I've shared mine with you. Some of those stories are stories of triumph some are of struggle. Sometimes young people reach out because they feel I've given them something and they want to give back. But I don't ask for anything in return, all I ever hope for is that you've learned something from reading this or hearing me speak and you keep it with you, and you use it.

A student who saw me speak years ago is also comedian in Vancouver. We started chatting at an open mic one night. I asked her what she is doing now after graduation besides comedy. Turned out she is an engineer, working with the Rick Hansen Foundation and had access to a team of people doing research with an exoskeleton suit. An exoskeleton suit is a robotic device that enables people with mobility issues to get up and walk. She connected me with the people working with the suit. I showed up at the Blussion Centre at Vancouver General Hospital a place where I was told many years before that I would never walk again. I showed up to "just get fitted and do a preliminary range of mobility tests before I could get up in the suit" and by some stroke of luck the next thing I know I have been given the green light to try it out that day. That day I took my first steps in seventeen years. That day I walked across a room and back. Something I never ever thought I would do again. And I love sharing this story.

I love sharing this story because I see it as such a great reminder to NEVER EVER give up hope. I never did. I still haven't. But even better than that. My favorite part of this story is who made those steps happen? It was a student, a young adult, like most of you reading this, helped me, a paralyzed man take his first steps in seventeen years. A young adult who saw me in her school speaking years before like so many thousands of others. She came back into my life and made my little sister Hayley's wish of seeing her big brother walk again come true. One person did that. One person made mine and my entire family's dream come true. And it makes me think of how many thousands of people have heard me speak and how many thousands more will read this book just how much potential there is between all of us to help others, to give back, to provide inspiration and support and love. To make this world a better place for all of us to live in.

And I truly want to thank all of you for everything you've given me, even just being here. Remember your potential is immeasurable so follow your dreams. Just be good people and look out for one another. And never lose hope. And if you ever need to come back and get a "pick-me-up", just open this book , wiggle your toes and remember this story.

AND AFTER

The last photo taken of me standing

My amazing family.

Friends

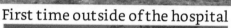

First time outside of the hospital

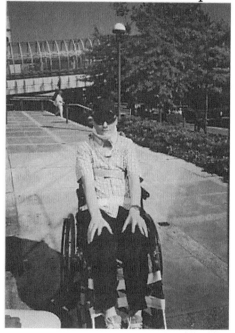

My greatest joy. Being in front of all of you

The lasting impression left on students

Featured: Abby

Dedicated to Brendon
Seen here with my sisters, Allison & Hayley

7

Abigail: Kevin Saved My Life That Day

*"It was a Friday at the end of March that I figured would be
the day that I died"*

I had a very difficult middle school experience. I was a
loner, I stuck to myself, usually to read. It didn't help that I went
through the awkward puberty stage before everyone else either. I
was the chunky, introvert with pimples that no one wanted to be
friends with. I got bullied every day. Multiple times a day about
my weight, my acne, my curly hair basically you name it, and
someone made fun of me for it. Kids are mean. I didn't have a lot
of friends and it was really hard. This was a time in my life where
you really need people the most. It's the time where you start to
form your friend groups that will carry over into adult life, and
it's also the time that you're starting to like boys and want to be
able to speak to your friends about that. But I didn't have that.
Instead it felt like everyone was against me. This all started for
me in about sixth or seventh grade, so I must've been about 12
or 13 years old and it went on until I graduated high school. And
it never got easier. As you get older kids get meaner. At one point
someone developed a Facebook group page entitled "Abby should
kill herself." That was a good one.

Obviously, I didn't because I'm here with you today, but oh
boy, did I want to. That moment in time was probably one of the

hardest things I've ever experienced. To know that people "hate" you so much, that they want to see you die, it's just such an awful feeling. And I was only in sixth grade at that point, I was still just a kid And this was a constant thing, this abuse. I would walk down the hallway and kids would knock my books out of my hands and call me "flabby Abby", just making fun of me for my weight or anything they could think of at the time. This happened every day.

I couldn't wait to get home every day. My family is amazing, they are loving and easy to talk to, same goes for my sister, so it was my solace at night, but it only carried over until the next morning when I'd have to wake up and dread every minute of the day ahead. I could never really get away from it. But it wasn't all bad, later that year I had my first boyfriend. It wasn't too serious because let's face it we were still in middle school. Nothing is ever too serious then. When we broke up it seemed sad and heart breaking at the time. It felt like the end of the world, looking back now I see how silly that is. But what did make it harder was that everyone made fun of me for it. I was already hurting over the loss of my young relationship and now I had everyone in school just kicking me some more while I'm already down. At that point, things just went downhill. I didn't know what depression was, I didn't know that what I was feeling wasn't just sadness, but it was actually diagnosable depression. This is also something that runs in my family, so I'm a little surprised that I didn't know about this hereditary trait. The hardest thing when going through depression is to have an outlet and I didn't have one. I played sports but it wasn't enough to help me kick these feelings. And then I got the idea for self-harm, and that was it. Cutting became my outlet.

It started with just scratching and pinching, then escalated to cutting, burning and bruising myself. And this was my way of dealing with things. I don't know why it made me feel better, but it did. Probably because it allowed me to feel "something" at the very least. And this became my coping mechanism for the time being. It was something that I could control. In a world where everything seemed lost, I actually had control over something. I could control the physical pain when the emotional pain became too much. This all started for me when I was about twelve years old and continued on all the way until high school, and things progressively got worse. I went to a single town middle school, but my high school was a culmination of five other towns. And even with all these new faces and new opportunities for friendships, I was still the quiet awkward loner that sat alone at lunch time. Between August and September, I found myself self-injuring more often. It went from only cutting on days that I felt overly sad and depressed and then as I entered high school, I found myself cutting in the morning, and then again at night. I felt isolated and alone. And it's never a good feeling.

As we entered high school the few friends that I did have suddenly changed. Before they would say "Hi" in the hallways, we would talk and joke around and now they became too cool in high school and my own friends turned on me because I was an easy victim. My friends began bullying me and laughing at me in the hallways, joining in with others as well. I already had chronic pain in my legs and had visited doctors all through growing up, so when people would make fun of me for the way I walked they didn't understand that I was in serious pain. The only thing that made me feel better emotionally would be to get outside and run around but that would trigger my leg pain and in turn I would cut myself to distract one pain from the other. I remember one instance where my closest friend growing up turned on me. She was the only person I would confide in outside of my family, and she knew the internal battles I had, not with depression but with the physical issues. I was walking through the cafeteria one day and I remember seeing her with her new group of friends, and I started heading that way. As I got closer, I heard that they were laughing at me the entire time. I thought before they were just talking to each other about something funny but my "best friend" was the one making fun of me the most to this new group of friends and they were all laughing at me. That was the last friend I had at the time, and now I was completely alone. That was a particularly hard day.

Other than that, I remember the feelings of being unwelcome and not really having anywhere to go. I began eating my lunch in the library after that. I can't pinpoint the exact moment I first decided that I wanted to end my life, but I was definitely there that year. I didn't see a point in continuing any further, and I felt like I was a burden to my family. It was also at this point where I started to develop a plan for how I was going to do it. As I said before my cutting was typically on my legs or upper arms or even on my abdomen where people couldn't see it, but as I got more and more depressed it came down to my forearms, usually underneath the arms and closer to my wrists. I also got to a point where I didn't care how deep I cut into my wrist, I didn't care if I was close to a vein, I didn't care how it looked or how bad it felt. I just didn't care if it all ended right then and there. I was reckless. What I didn't realize was that in doing so, I would get more depressed and this would make me feel more isolated and it was just a constant hole that I was in and instead of climbing out I was digging myself in deeper. I wasn't communicating with anyone not even my family at this point.

It was Friday at the end of March, that I decided would be the day that I die. I got up that morning feeling good, knowing what I was about to do that day. I went to school and cleaned out my locker so that way my parents wouldn't have to do it later. And my plan was as soon as I got home, I would cut deep enough that it would kill me this time. In knowing what I had planned I felt a strange sense of Zen that whole morning. I didn't care about class, but I didn't feel sad, I just didn't feel anything. I just couldn't wait to get home and do what I had planned. It was then that the teacher told us we had an assembly to go to, I figured it was no big deal just go sit in the auditorium and zone out for an hour and it was one hour closer to my time.

They introduced the speaker that day and it was this guy

who they said was a drunk driver and got into an accident. At first, I thought "cool, I don't have my license or my permit, so this doesn't even relate to me. And at this point I'm never going to have either so it's totally pointless for me to pay attention." But when Kevin came into the room it just felt different, you felt the aura change in the room as silly as it may sound to some people, but it did. I decided to listen to his story. I listened as he told us about his life and what he's been through. A friend of his died because of him, the family he destroyed, the paralysis he feels, he can't walk, he can't even pee anymore without help. He talked about how he was depressed and his thoughts of suicide. He talked about this and it was then that it clicked. He's here. He's still here. How can someone go through this much tragedy and still be here? And for the first time I felt like I wasn't alone. Someone else knew the feelings and was able to get through it.

I began to think about my own situation. I thought about how I would feel sorry for myself or would curl up and stay locked in my room not trying to fix my situation. The main problem I think with depression and suicide is that no one is talking about it. And now I was here listening to someone tell their story and their feelings and it was honestly such a relief to know that it wasn't something wrong with me. I went on to find out my grandfather had struggled with it, but that was a time when no one really knew what to do about it, they just chalked it up to you feeling sad. But finally, someone understood me. And it made me really feel like an asshole. I may not have any friends; I may struggle with being alone or dealing with chronic pain but that's it. That's all that's wrong with me. And after hearing Kevin speak, well, that was me. A huge asshole. I realized then that I needed to get it together. My life is not as bad I think it is. Kevin told us how he hit rock bottom, he should have been dead, lost all use of his body and he STILL got it together and turned something so awful so atrocious into something positive that people could learn from. I was pretty ashamed of myself. I felt selfish. I felt stupid. How could my issues seem so big? I went through the rest of the day totally numb. I hadn't felt anything in a really long time and now for the first time I felt "something" after seeing Kevin speak that day.

I went home after school that day and instead of picking up the blades and cutting myself, I threw them all in the trash. I threw away anything else that day that I would've used in the past to self-harm myself and I reached out to Kevin via email. I told him about my history, I told him about the cutting and suicidal thoughts. I also told him that that day seeing him changed my life. And he saved my life. Within 24 hours he responded to me. He told me how amazing it was that I got it out of his story. His response was very genuine and very heartfelt, I definitely felt cared for, even from a complete stranger but also in a way we understood each other. He told me that he had friends of his commit suicide and the struggles he went through with that and how it affected those around them. We continued talking here and there after that day. He recommended that I reach out to the woman that coordinated his speech at the school that day, and she could help me find a therapist. I did what he said, and he was right. The therapy sessions were a huge benefit to my mental health and keeping me on the straight and narrow path.

The only negative moment I had after that day, was from my best friend. We had rekindled our relationship and were very close again. I even let her read my letter to Kevin so she could understand my feelings and how I felt that she hurt me. I also wanted someone to talk to. Someone I could be myself, and not a therapist but a friend. She was not that person. She told everyone in the school about my feelings and my depression. She told teachers, guidance counselors, basically anyone who would listen and then the police got involved and called my mom. The thing is I wasn't even suicidal anymore, I was proud of my recovery process and wanted to have a friend by my side. But this wasn't the right friend. Luckily, I told my sister prior to her finding out through the grapevine. I do remember when I got home that day having to explain to my mom what was going on in my head. And that was an extremely difficult conversation to have with your parents. The look in their eyes is easily enough to break your heart.

My mom can't imagine a day on earth without me here, and here I was about to selfishly do that to her. But I know that I would not be here without Kevin. And luckily, I was able to stay in contact with him and share my journey of healing with him. And I'm definitely a different person now, ten years later I couldn't imagine being the same person I was then. He also helped keep me stay sane when I had leg surgery, I was placed into a wheelchair for six months. And it was definitely a feeling of helplessness, but he reassured me that you should never focus on what you can't do but instead what you can do. And he's right those little moments like wiggling your toes it seems so small but it's something we take for granted. Years later, I joined a host of others who honored Kevin by getting the "Just Wiggle Your Toes" tattoo on my foot. I'm not confident that I would have made it through any of these surgeries, or low points in my life had it not been for meeting him that one day, I really can't stress how hanging on for one more day can really change everything.

Now ten years later, I still live in Vermont, I have great friends, great support and I met my current fiancé about four years ago now and we are about to close on our own house. We have a great relationship with very open communication. I've told him about the depression and suffering and I still have those moments where I feel down, but in those moments, I've realized that I've grown, and I can talk about it. I know I can invest that time in myself, I don't owe anyone else but myself for my well-being. So, I'll go for a run, I'll sit outside in the park, I'll give my dog some extra love. It's not a light switch you turn off but instead you learn to deal with it and change your mood on your own. Currently, I work in a bank and its very stressful. Some days I find myself having a tough time, I'll just sit in my car for twenty minutes before I drive home, or I'll spend a little alone time and do something I enjoy and if you just vocalize that to people, they will understand. I think people just need to know you aren't mad at them, you aren't ignoring them, you just are working on a little "me time." And it's not selfish, but just communicate. You will always have people in your corner but at the end of the day it really is only up to you to make that change. And you CAN do it. I never thought I could have the life I have now. I don't know what the future holds for me now, but I think that one day I would love to have my own children. Not right now. I have some big travel plans ahead of me. It's a big world out there with so much to see and experience.

And I'm here. I'm alive. And I want to experience as much as I possibly can. There's so much joy out there and there's so much life to live.

8

Chelsea: Loneliness and Depression

"I felt abandoned. I felt as if I wasn't worthy of love from anyone at that point."

When I was six years old, I lost my father in a fatal car accident. My mother, who was in recovery, turned to drugs again to help cope with the pain and didn't go back to treatment for many years. I was moved in with my grandparents at that point and although they were great, they weren't my parents. I know now that this led to a lot of attachment issues growing up and would make me overcompensate in certain relationships. Which in turn would lead to me having less friends, except maybe for the odd two or three. All through elementary school, I struggled with my identity and as to where I belonged. My mother literally abandoned me, and my father was dead, I felt like I didn't have any placement, I didn't belong to anybody.

Getting into the teenage years is tough for everyone especially when transitioning into high school. The whole environment changes. School was never my friend, I never looked forward to waking up in the morning and walking to school. At the start of grade eight I started going through some very depressive episodes. I couldn't cope with my feelings of loneliness. Even though I had a good family life and a few good friends, it just didn't seem fulfilling. It could also be because I saw my friends and their home lives with their mom and dad. I didn't have that. It made me feel shut off, like, I just didn't fit in. Around thirteen or fourteen years old I started to become angry. I remember telling my mother on multiple occasions to never talk to me again, and I didn't want her in my life. I didn't realize how much words like this can hurt people. My grandmother told me one day that I needed to watch what I said, because my words can cause real actions. My grandmother was worried that my emotional rage would set my mom off, and there was a chance she would purposely overdose to kill herself. So, I started bottling up my anger. I wasn't happy but I didn't want to hurt anyone else. I was a horrible daughter, at least I felt so. I wasn't good enough, and I couldn't get out of this downward spiral. This is also when I started cutting.

I didn't start cutting in order to kill myself or necessarily because I wanted to die but more so because I was angry. I was angry at my mom for what she did, and what she didn't do by taking care of me. I just had bottled up all my feelings and all my anger and needed something to give me release. It wasn't until the start of grade nine that those feelings had escalated, and I started having suicidal thoughts. Would anyone notice if I was gone? Would anyone even care? The thoughts crossed my mind more and more. Thinking back to it now, it happened so many times I don't even want to tell you the number of times I felt that way. I never had an exact plan for how I wanted to do it, but I did know I didn't want to be here anymore. I felt like I was a burden to my family. If it wasn't for me, my grandparents wouldn't have had to give up their retirement plans to now raise another set of children. I felt like my mother didn't love me and had abandoned me. I felt like I wasn't worthy of love from anyone at that point.

These thoughts led me into a really dark period that I couldn't cheer myself out of. Then I heard about Kevin Brooks speaking at schools. He had not come to my school recently, but I learned about him through some friends that heard him speak. I was inspired by his story and wanted to see him. He looked like he had been through a lot, but made it out strong. I needed to know how he did it. Around halfway through grade nine I pretty much had it with living. I never told anyone my feelings. Not my family not my friends. Had I done that I feel like I would've had an amazing support group, but I also didn't want them to treat me differently and treat me like a victim.

I decided I would reach out to Kevin, he's a stranger, he doesn't know me. If he answered, cool. If not, not a problem I would continue on with my plan. I told him I wanted to meet him and hear his story. To my shock, he responded within 24 hours. He actually told me that he was speaking at my school in a couple of months, and to hang in there. We continued talking, and as the date got closer, I asked my school administrators what grade Kevin would be speaking to. It turned out; he wasn't speaking to my class but to the year ahead instead. I felt defeated. I really wanted to hear this speech, I wanted to meet him, I wanted to feel hope, and just get pulled out of the rut I'm in. But they told me I couldn't go. I reached back out to Kevin and told him what happened. I also relayed to him some of my darkest secrets about my feelings. I told him about my suicidal thoughts, something I never told anyone before. I remember he said, "You are a priority and I'm here for you." That felt amazing. No one has ever made me feel like that. I remember one time I even emailed him, and he responded right away and said "I'm traveling and about to get on a plane, but I want you to know I hear you and I'm here for you, I'll get back to you as soon as I can." Just even those moments, they seem so insignificant, but when you feel like no one cares and the world is over. Those moments really hit you hard. Someone cares.

As the time of his presentation arrived, I begged the school administrators to let me in, eventually they relented, and I remember sitting in the auditorium just in awe. Most other kids don't even pay attention, I mean we were teenagers and we were just happy to not be in class at the moment. But I will tell you, when he speaks, they really listen. For me, it was hard to hear all the words, I spent most of his presentation sobbing to myself in my seat in the back. After the crowd cleared, I walked up to him, and introduced myself. And he just hugged me. And I really felt loved. This guy, who went through so much, and lived through so much with such little mobility then why can't I? I have freedom. I have abilities. My life is not that bad and it's not over. He told me some more personal stories of his struggles, and to be honest I don't know how he does it. I'm not that strong, and if I were in his shoes, I probably wouldn't want to be alive. I went home that day and looked at the pocketknife, now a bit embarrassed for my actions. The habit of cutting didn't stop immediately because it was also an addiction, but it did stop shortly thereafter.

We continued talking off and on for the next two years. Every time he had a presentation at my school, I would get permission to go and see him. Our friendship now had grown to a brother/sister bond, and we would go to dinners and hang out. He was always an email away or a text away, I could tell him I was having a hard day and he would understand. He has two younger sisters, so I think he just adopted me as one of his own. And it was really nice, because now for the first time I really felt like I belonged.

Around grade twelve I decided that I needed to get some actual medical help and he was supportive throughout the process. Asking for that help really changed my life, some people just need to have medication. There's nothing wrong with you, it's just a little boost to your attitude. I understand asking for it is hard, and maybe embarrassing but you'd be surprised what a difference it makes and once you're living that difference you don't feel embarrassed at all. You're too busy feeling good. Kevin is not judgmental, and he talked me through that decision and its one of the best decisions I ever made in my life, besides not ending my life of course.

I'm twenty six years old now and mother to a four year-old boy. I have a career now and am slowly working my way to becoming a counselor, so I can help others feel stronger and make it to a happier tomorrow. It's been twelve years since I first met Kevin Brooks, we are still friends and he means everything to me. I wanted to kill myself at fourteen years old and here I am still living. Kevin is a reminder to me that I can keep going, he is a reminder that in your darkest state he is the hope that you see and the voice that you hear pulling you to the light. Life still has its ups and downs, and I still call him during tough times. My mother passed away this past year, I told him, and he reassured me that he will always be a there for me and that I wasn't alone. He taught me so much over the years. He taught me that no matter what happens, you can overcome. That no matter how tough things may seem - it IS ok to reach out and ask for help. You can't really understand what someone's breaking point is. My worst moment is maybe not so bad for you, and your worst may not be so bad for me, so I get it, it's hard to understand.

I think people just have to realize that we are all different. Different things affect us all in different ways. Kevin taught me its ok to change things though on a small scale. One small step, no pun intended there, but one small thing you can control each day. It's a move in the right direction and eventually all those small steps will add up to one big change. His slogan "Just Wiggle Your Toes" is something I would remember when I didn't have the energy to make that one small step. It was something that reminded me that I was alive, and I was able to make a change. Some days you just don't feel like it, and that's ok, but knowing that you at least have the ability to means a lot. He's been in that dark place just like I was, and he's still here. If he can do it, so can I. His continued support through the years has really changed my life. And there's days I still feel out of control but knowing that tomorrow will come, and you can recover is all I really need.

No matter how dark times can seem and how out of control it can get, stop, take a breath, and just wiggle your toes.

9

Kevin: Where Would I Be Now?
And How Did I Get Here?

*"All the things you struggle to succeed in life while having
a fully capable body, seemed all that more implausible now
that I was paralyzed."*

So, when I was about 15 years old, my dad got me a job
in the gravel pit where he and my grandfather both worked as
well. My dad just retired from there about three years ago, so it
was definitely a family business to work for Jack Cewe Gravel. In
school, I wasn't really an academic student. But I wasn't dumb either. I just didn't have any real interest in what was being taught,
and I found more pleasure just skateboarding, smoking pot and
causing trouble. Now, again, let me reiterate this book should
teach you what not to do. Anyway, going to class just wasn't a priority for me, so I kind of just scraped by school, grades wise. And
I had no plans of going to college or University. So, my dad got me
this job at the gravel pit. It was the crappiest job ever. At first.

I would climb up big mountains of gravel every day. Meanwhile a conveyer belt was running overhead and just pelting me
with ¾ inch rocks constantly onto my hard hat. Every so often
I would take one to the face. Man, does that sting and wake you
up quickly first thing in the morning. My job at the pit was to
pick the wooden twigs out of the gravel as they fell to the ground.

Reason being, when they make the gravel into concrete it can't have any wood in it. So, that's how I spent my days, just climbing up and down gravel hills and picking up twigs. My next big job was hosing off the scales that the dump-trucks drove over. I liked that job just because I could tell people I got paid to be a hoser. So Canadian eh? Then I moved up to a painter position. I would spend my days painting machinery or the massive water tanks that were on site. I probably enjoyed that the most. Until the next summer when I met Tom.

Tom was the resident electrician. A Scotsman with white curly hair, beard to match and jovial laugh, he was just awesome to be around. And I really enjoyed my time working with him in the electrical field. I realized, I really liked working at the pit. Mostly because of my family legacy there. I was Jim's kid. That gained me an instant "in". Even when I had a blue mohawk, jeans fifteen sizes too big and a hoody pulled over my head in the dead heat of summer so that I could hide my headphones and listen to punk rock while I worked. Yeah, that freak. Regardless of my appearance I was a hard worker and a Brooks. So everyone treated me very well.

I liked to work with my hands, I liked being outdoors I really thought that this could be it. This could be my future right here in front of me. I had never really thought about doing anything otherwise as a career besides maybe dreaming of being in the NHL. But that dream had long since passed. In my mind at this point, a job was something you did to earn a living and provide for yourself and eventually a family and it was a bonus if you didn't hate it. I was making good money. Definitely more than any of my friends. There were benefits and room for advancement. This was a good career for me should I stick with it. Unfortunately, that's about the time I got laid off. So, until work picked up again there, I was forced to go and do odd jobs to make money. At the time of the crash I was working for this company selling these new devices called cell phones, as a shipping driver. I also worked at a restaurant as a server. For fun, I got back into playing hockey and was playing in a men's league just below the restaurant where I worked. I didn't mind these jobs but I also didn't see myself sticking around longer than I had to, especially if work picked back up at the gravel pit. I was essentially just passing the time, earning enough money to have fun, put gas in my car and hit the mountains with my snowboard as often as possible. I was taking some evening courses to make up for all the messing around I did in high school. As much as I regretted not just getting it done when I was, you know, in high school, I will admit that Math 11 is much easier the third time around. My big plan was to get into British Columbia Institute of Technology and begin my apprenticeship back at the pit once I had the necessary skills and work became available again. Had it not been for the car crash, I think it is safe to say I could very well still working at the pit. In the very least I would be an electrician.

How I found myself speaking in schools is a total random act of coincidence.

After the crash and my new life with a wheelchair, my dad sold his house because of all of the stairs. There were stairs to get into the house, stairs to get to my room, it was not conducive to my new life, so I was forced to move into a small apartment with my mom. Her place was nice, but it was tiny. She had to move all her stuff out of her room and into basically a den which had previously served as Hayley's room. So they bunked up together and I rolled into the big room, as it was the only room that I could physically roll into. It was tricky to maneuver around that apartment in my chair. The hallways were narrow. I couldn't turn my wheelchair around in the bathroom because it was so tight. It was extremely frustrating. But this was my life now. A life I surely hadn't planned on. But a life I was determined to figure out.

Coming home and leaving the wheelchair accessible environment that was GF Strong was somewhat of a rude awakening. Going anywhere and doing anything was a momentous task.

Physically, it was easiest to just stay home inside. But I am a person who loves being outdoors. I needed fresh air, exercise and adventure. I could look outside and see the world through our 4th floor window. It looked as it always had before. The world hadn't changed, I had. It was evident that the world also wasn't going to change for me. So my options were that I could either give up or I could learn to adapt.

One day, home alone and bored, I decided I needed to get outside. Out the door, right turn, twenty five pushes to the elevator, push the button, roll in and go down. Right turn, out the elevator, fifteen pushes to the front door, park to the left of the heavy glass door and grab the handle on the right and pull hard. Now quickly sneak my chair out the opening before the door slams shut on me. A quick bump over the threshold of the door and I was outside. I would map out every detail of my travel. I had to. There were obstacles everywhere. I tried my best not to let it get to me. I tried looking at it like skateboarding. I had to find my line. My path of travel. If I could add a wheelie or a curb hop into the mix, sick. I might as well try to have some fun in this chair. On this day I made it to the elevator but it was not responding to my requests for a ride down. It turns out new people were moving in and they had locked the elevator for their convenience. There was no way to communicate this to my new neighbors. At least I thought so at first. I wracked my brain for a plan. I needed a strategy. I got it. I rolled into the staircase and began yelling "Hello. HELLO!!" my voice echoed through the concrete corridor and spiraled down the stairs. No response. Ok, then. I guess this is on me. I turned my chair around 180 degrees and backed it up just to the edge of the staircase behind me. I grabbed each cold metal hand railing on either side with each hand and leaned my body as far forward as I possibly could. Then one by one, I bumped my chair backwards down each step. There must have been twelve steps per staircase and four staircases in total. Man, was it loud. Clunk, Clunk, SMASH. Clunk, Clunk, SMASH!! My descent was so jarring that it must have caught the attention of the people moving in. They came running into the stairwell to see what the commotion was. To their horror, I am sure, the commotion was a man rolling down multiple flights of stairs backwards in a wheelchair. They apologized embarrassingly and offered to unlock the elevator for me. An offer to which I politely declined. For one, I figured that this would teach them a lesson never to lock an elevator again. Also, I was quite proud of myself for overcoming this seemingly insurmountable challenge. And off I went. Clunk, Clunk, SMASH! Clunk, Clunk, SMASH! See ya!!

I slowly mapped out paths of travel around my new neighborhood. I often refer to my brain as a GPS of accessibility. Rolling down the sidewalk to the curb, cut and across the street to Superstore – Canada's version of Walmart; then past Superstore to Sammy J Peppers a trendy restaurant I was fond of; then past Sammy J's to Fitness World, the gym I would soon join. Before the crash I was never interested in the gym. I was physically fit and had a lot of other outdoor activities. I never saw the appeal of exercising indoors with weights and machines. Now, with all of my pastimes gone, the gym was the one place where I could release my endorphins. A place where I could work up a sweat and pound out my frustration. I took to it immediately. I went almost every day. I loved the staff at Fitness World too. Everyone was super kind to me. When I was done with my work out I would always crush a protein shake at the snack bar and chat with the guy who ran it. I'd ask questions about protein and muscle gain. Who is this guy? I am gym guy now? I was all in. After my shake and feeling jacked I would roll out of the gym and all the way back to my mom's apartment. I started to pound that roll home out like it was nothing. No more struggle. No more pain. No more breaks. The stronger I got the less arduous the day-to-day tasks like dressing, bathing and travelling became. I was gaining independence. Glorious independence. My own personal Stanley Cup. I was twenty two years old. I needed my freedom.

Maybe it's genetics. Maybe it's because both of my parents

were active people and instilled that in their kids, but being physically active just came naturally to us Brooks kids. Sure, I was working with less muscle and moving body parts, but I was finding ways to get around and feeling good about myself.

I did my best to keep my days busy. If I stayed busy I didn't have to think about the crash or Brendon and his grieving family. I didn't have to think about Robyn or my broken heart, not being at the skateboard park with my friends or my broken body. I could temporarily forget about my totaled car or how I would provide for myself for the rest of my life. I found some purpose and fulfillment in overcoming the barriers that surrounded me. The mission of basic survival distracted me from the reality of what lay ahead in the weeks, months and years before me. When I would get home and settle in for the night is when I would struggle the most with my thoughts. I was twenty two years old, life was just beginning. Or it was supposed to be. Almost everything I loved was gone. I hated feeling sorry for myself. It seemed so selfish. How could I complain? I was still here. My thoughts always went to Brendon's family. What were they going through today? But the heart is a strong muscle and it pulls hard. I remember thinking no one is going to ever be with me again because of this wheelchair. Who could love someone in a wheelchair? How was I going to be able to work? How would I maintain relationships with my buddies when the skatepark and the mountains seemed as far away as the moon?

To further complicate things I was still a kid. I haven't had enough life experience yet. I haven't been through anything remotely as tragic or difficult as this experience before to know that I could get through this. I hadn't faced real adversity until now. Sure, I had faced hard times. Many of which were jams I had put myself into with other poor decisions, but I had also bounced back from those lows. I always somehow landed on my feet. How was I supposed to bounce back from this? I felt incomplete. A brain trapped in a barely mobile body. I was lost in so many ways and just trying to keep my brain occupied just enough that I could stay an arm's reach away from the darkness of depression. Away from the overwhelming weight of what had happened. I would lay in bed at night unable to sleep. Thoughts racing through my mind. A future so uncertain. It was difficult to look far forward. I didn't know where I was going or how I would get there or if I even wanted to get there. I didn't want any of this. I was making do as best I could. But for how long could I just make do? There was a long life ahead and living it in a wheelchair was not something I wanted to accept. I'd try to move my legs. It was like trying to move a pencil across a table with my mind. I could visualize my legs moving. They just wouldn't move. It felt like my brain was getting the messages through my nerve endings all the way to my toes, and when I would try to move the nerves were responding deep down inside. They just weren't strong enough to move my heavy legs. Heavy like concrete. Concrete void of twigs just as there was likely a new stick boy at Jack Cewe. Oh, how I would love to climb one of those gravel mountains. I'd take a million rocks to the face to not be trapped in this damaged body. I would try to wiggle my toes. I would sit up and grab each toe with my fingers and try to wiggle them. Hoping for a flicker. A twitch. Anything. Nothing. I had occasional thoughts of suicide, but I had no intentions of ever following through with these thoughts. That would be the easy way out and so unfair to everyone who loved me. But how do you live while knowing that another person is dead because of your choices?

There were nights I would cry. Cry myself to sleep. Wishing I could go back in time. Wishing I could take away all of the pain and go back to how things were. Why did I do this? How could I be so reckless to just throw away so much for something so stupid as driving drunk. I knew it was wrong when I did it. It wasn't like I didn't know better or didn't have options to get home safe that night. But there was no going back. I could drive myself crazy thinking of things I could have done differently, but the sad reality was no matter how hard I wished or how hard I tried I could not reverse what had happened. I made the choices. I would live forever with the consequences. This was my bed. And I would lay in it struggling to grasp the brutal truth that this was my life now.

I dealt with the emotions as best I could. I had a pen and notebook beside my bed and I would write songs. I preferred calling them songs. Songs sounded cooler than poems. Somehow putting words that rhymed to paper was therapeutic. I would work for hours on these songs. I would count the syllables and create the rhythm. I would read and rewrite every single word until I had it just right. Writing kept me sane in those late lonely nights. I was obsessed with finding the ideal words to convey what I was going through and how I felt. I would stay up until the sun rose in order to write the perfect song. Only when I had completed these songs could my brain shut off and allow me to sleep. Mentally exhausted from my thoughts of the evening and physically exhausted from the activities I would perform in the day to escape my thoughts, I would eventually fall asleep. Sometimes, in my dreams, I was still walking. Sometimes, I was in a wheelchair. I would almost always get out of the wheelchair. Slowly at first. I would move one leg and then the other and then slowly stand up. One step, two steps. I'd jump to make sure I still had stability. Run to ensure that I had maintained agility. I'd run as fast as I could. I would feel free again. I would think it was all just a dream. Elated, I would rush to the nearest skateboard shop and buy a board, griptape, trucks, bearings and wheels. I would eagerly watch the skateboarder who worked at the shop start to assemble my new board. Levitating with excitement. Everything was back to normal. I would never screw this up again. It was just a dream. Then, I would wake up. I would wake up to the nightmare. The same nightmare over and over. Dreading the day ahead. And like salt to the wound, outside my window were blue skies, birds chirping and the sound of a skateboard going down the sidewalk - Clack! Clack! Clack! A seemingly beautiful day. Maybe for everyone else, but not for me How am I going to do this again? How am I going to get through another day? Defeated, I would turn my head over and just stare blankly at the wall. Completely defeated. But there, beside me on my bedstand was my notepad and the song I had anguished over the night before. My song. I would read those words. Over and over. I found peace from those words those rhythms, those rhymes. I found meaning and joy in turning despair into poetry. I found inspiration in turning destruction into creation. Negativity into something positive. My songs gave me strength and motivation to face another day ahead. Words were my savior. One word at a time. One song at a time. One day at a time.

One of these days I found myself across the street at the Superstore just grabbing odds and ends, when a group of teenage skater kids approached me. They asked what happened and how I wound up in a wheelchair. So, I went into my story with them. I was used to telling my story to strangers at this point. It's actually surprising how many people would just come up and straight up ask me what happened. I didn't always feel like sharing my darkest most difficult moments of my life with random people so often times I would just tell those who asked that I was attacked by an elk, and quickly roll away. Let them think about that for a minute. But with the skater kids I felt like these were my people and I could tell they were genuinely interested. They were probably expecting some story of a gnarly skating accident or something but that's of course not what they heard. I told them I was drunk driving and speeding in my car after a party. I told them that I had crashed and woke up and that my friend had died and that I was paralyzed. I told them that I used to skate and snowboard and that I missed both so much. They hung on every word. I can't say that I had any greater motive to begin with than answering their question that they asked me. But after I was done sharing it with them and they skated off I could still see their faces; I can still see them today. They heard me. I thought in that moment these kids will never drink and drive. Great! Whether they did or not I will never know, but that experience gave me an idea to use the one thing I did have at my disposal... My voice.

Not long after that encounter with the skater kids in Super-store across from my mom's apartment had I taken on a new pro-ject. A chance meeting with a man named Rick Hansen had set me on a path to swim across a lake and hold a fundraiser. I was training and gathering gifts for sponsors and gathering donations from donors, trying to learn what the heck I was doing all at the same time. Fortunately, I had a great team of support around me. The lake swim was a huge success. Not long after myself and a guy named Joel who had swam with me and coincidentally had gotten in a crash in the same intersection as Brendon and I. He too, had crashed causing paralysis to half his body. We were in-vited to speak at an elementary school where Joel's mom worked. Looking back, if I had to sum that first talk up with one word it would be "awkward." I had no idea what I was doing. No plan really of what I was going to say. Just a half an hour of speaking time, a library full of maybe grade three and four students and a video cassette with news footage from the swim. A teacher even told me after the talk that the next time around I should plan out what I was going to say first. Not bad advice. I just didn't expect there to be a next time, but low and behold there was.

Around this time a friend of mine named Angela was work-ing in a nearby city to where I was living called Abbotsford. She had just finished her public relations diploma at Kwantlen Col-lege and was working on a program called Safer Cities. One of the main partners was an organization called ICBC which stands for the Insurance Corporation of British Columbia. If you drive in BC you go through ICBC. ICBC also has a road safety speaker program and sponsor talks at high schools across the province. Angela mentioned to a man named Don, who worked for ICBC, what I was doing in schools. Soon we were having lunch together discussing my potential inclusion in the program. Angela deserves credit here because not only did she introduce me to Don but she also suggested that I take the Public Relations program which led me to meeting Rick Hansen which led to the swim which led to me starting speaking. Thanks Angela!!!

My first talks with ICBC were terrifying. A classroom full of elementary school kids was one thing, but an entire gymnasium packed with teenagers... Come on! Terrifying. I remember writing out my speech word for word sitting by the window in my mom's apartment. Memories of grade eleven English class were rushing to my head, of me turning beet red in front of the class while attempting to talk about I can't remember what... A book I had to read or something. I was trembling so hard that the paper I was holding was impossible to read. So embarrassing. How was I going to do this? How would I hold all of pages still for 45 minutes!? Ok, scratch that. No more paper. I know this story. I lived it. I won't say that I wasn't nervous at that first school, or the next, and the next and the next after that. It's not as hard to speak in front of a people when you are telling a personal story and not trying to remember someone else's. I also remember feeling a lot more comfortable sitting down speaking to a crowd than standing up. How convenient.

Before long I was travelling across the province with ICBC and then soon after was getting invited across the country. Alberta and Saskatchewan were my first province conferences with small school tours to follow. It was cool to go to these places I had never been, and to my surprise be relatable. For some reason in the early days of speaking I figured if I was beyond my own area code or home province people would not understand the story because they didn't know exactly where it had happened. But the thing is these kinds of stories happen everywhere. Small towns, big cities doesn't matter. Crashes are killing young people all over the world because that combination of inexperience, invincibility and a tendency to risky behavior that many young people have is a very dangerous combination. A deadly one, sadly, in many cases.

About ten years into my travels across Canada I met Cara and her husband Jason. Cara is a speaker with a powerful story of her own about her twin sister dying in a speed related motor vehicle crash just after their 18th birthday. Cara had travelled the world speaking and even had worked with speaking powerhouse, Tony Robbins. She also got her start with ICBC, like myself. Cara was kind enough to take me on as her first speaker in her speaker bureau The Drive To Save Lives and soon I was speaking all over the United States of America. New places, new faces, and my story was evolving to incorporate new messages too.

Now this is where I see the impact firsthand. And this is why I love doing physical talks in front of students.

Just outside of Edmonton Alberta, I had two huge presentations that day. A lot of times after the presentations students will approach me and sometimes it feels like everyone in the entire room. Sometimes they want to just give you high fives, or they promise to skateboard in my honor today. Basically, just thank you's and chit chat. But this one day, this student approached me, and was super emotional. She was trembling as she reached into her pocket to pull out a piece of paper, which this isn't uncommon, usually kids write me messages and hand them off as notes to me. But not today. Today this kid handed me this piece of paper, and as I opened it up a razor blade dropped out and fell to the floor. Then I read the note. It detailed how the student had planned on killing themselves that day and this was the razor blade they were going to use to do it. It went on to say, "You saved my life." I can't even comprehend the gravity of the situation when you're in that moment. This kid was looking at me, crying, crumbling to bits in front of me, and telling me how it has all changed because of me. I wrapped my arms around them and gave them the biggest hug knowing that in that moment that kid was safe. I kept the razor blade tight with me wrapped in that note until all of the students had gone back to class then I rolled out of the school and found a garbage can. I unwrapped the razor blade and disposed of it. I kept the note though. I keep these kinds of notes. My home is full of notes and cards and mementos that I have received over the years.

Before I drove away that day and onto the next town and school, I mentioned to the school counselor what was said, and this kid did get the help they needed. As long as somebody at the school knows and is aware of a struggling student in need, I can feel ok heading off to the next place, and as much as I want to keep in touch with every struggling soul out there it just is not possible. School counselors are saviors to me as much as they are to the kids that they help. I have actually been offered counseling positions at a number of schools over the years. I take that as a huge compliment but politely decline because I'm a travelling counsellor. I want to get to as many schools as I can and reach as many people as I can and help as many people as I possibly can. Another time I told a counselor about a student who was depressed who had confided in me. That student blew up in a rage. They were angry that I would say something to anyone, felt like I betrayed them. It's a fine line because they have confided in me, but I explain that legally I am obligated and that if I don't report them and something happens, I could never speak again and never help another troubled soul. Most who have been frustrated with me forgive me when they learn this. Years later, that same student messaged me and told me how thankful they were that I did that. They too got the help they needed and are in a much happier place. Depression, anxiety and suicide started to rival the messages I was getting about seatbelts, impaired driving, and speeding. Then one evening I got an email from a student that would change everything. Her name was Abigail. She was cutting herself and she didn't know why. I don't remember her telling me that she was suicidal. Maybe not in that first email. I was touched by her story, nonetheless. I just read her story again in full detail a couple hours ago while editing this book as I'm sure you just read it too. It's heartbreaking what she was going through. But it is also so inspiring what she went through and where she is today.

Abigail taught me about self-harm issues, and what real de-

pression feels like. I always had moments where I struggled growing up. My parents were divorced, I'd watch them argue, I would
get into trouble and I would self-sabotage and put myself in bad
situations. I never self-harmed. I'd just smashed stuff. Flip off a
teacher. Bully people. Claim my space as some kind of author-
ity. I guess it's similar in some ways. I wanted to project my pain
onto something else and see the reaction of a window breaking, a
teacher snapping, a person bleeding. Though breaking things was
maybe a temporary band-aid, and not one I recommended by any
means, it also got me in a ton more trouble which further con-
tributed to an already depressive mood that I was in. I started to
understand self-harmers just wanting to feel something. To see a
reaction. To take control of a situation that seems to be spiraling
away from them. They want to bleed out the pain and poison inside of them that is holding them back from happiness. To break
the numbing feeling that encompasses their every day. These kids
actually taught me so much, and from that I would delve deeper
into my own mind. It turns out we had a family history of depression as well, and I never would have known if these students
didn't share their stories with me and make me want to learn
more about their condition and in doing so make sense of my
own. I speak at this one school Port Moody Secondary every year
for at least the last ten years, and the counselor Dino who books
me is a beauty, I love the guy. So this is one of my favorite schools
that I look forward to speaking at every year that passes and I feel
it's fitting that it would be a student from this school who would
reach out years later and offer me the opportunity to take formal
training in what I had been sort of just winging all along. The organization is called IMAlive or IMAlive.org and it is a volunteer
run support network for people in crisis. I guess you could call it a
suicide prevention hotline. They do great work and I am so grateful that these kinds of resources exist. There are plenty of them,
and they are only a quick internet search away. IMAlive trained
me to be a better responder, which meant listening more than
offering advice and empowering more than trying to solve other
problems. Tools I use to this day to help be a better supporter. Yet

another student who sought me out and helped me be better at what I do. Thank You Hannah and IMAlive.

This made such a difference in my presentations. It became so much more powerful in every way. I could now better address those reaching out battling whatever demons they may be, and I had the tools to properly manage situations with resources to offer. My presentations changed from just being driver's safety to an all-encompassing roadmap of hope for kids who feel lost or broken at times. I didn't realize how much of an impact I made until a student approached me after a presentation at a high school in Winnipeg and asked me to sign "Just Wiggle Your Toes" on their wrist. I did it, and as I looked up there was a twenty to thirty person lineup behind him. Most of these students had scars on their wrists or arms from where they had self-harmed. Now, how could I not address this more often? Then I met Chelsea. She was in a dark place. Just how dark I didn't know at the time. I told her "Just hang on it'll get better." And luckily, eventually it did. It got better and here she is years later. I'm so proud of Chelsea. She has overcome so much and is dedicating her life and time to helping others who are less fortunate. I learned a lot of times it's about just being there for people. You don't have to have all the answers or come up with some huge conceptual plan, just be there for them and support them. Believe in them because they might not be in a place to be able to believe in themselves. Because sometimes that's all they want and that's all they need is just someone to hear them out and not judge them or lecture them. Maybe no one is giving that to them or they're too scared to talk to their friends and family. I hear it all the time where kids are uncomfortable talking about it and downplay their own feelings. Or even worse, sometimes they feel like they are a burden on those around them because of the way that they feel inside.

There's the old story of a kid telling his father he's depressed, and the dad says, "Shut up just play football, quit being a pussy." But it's not that easy. It's a real thing. It's a chemical imbalance in your brain. They don't have control over it, and it's a battle fighting against yourself. It sneaks in when you're vulnerable and it tells you lies like "You don't have anyone who cares, these medications won't help you, you're useless", but it's not true. These things really can destroy you. For me, I would think about the fact that I'm paralyzed so I felt useless. I also killed a friend of mine. So, I had two options, either give up or learn to fight. And I chose to fight from day one. Some setbacks and dark days along the way for sure, many of them still, but none I could not overcome. I am still here.

It was a struggle each day and some days I didn't win, but I tried. Some days it was a struggle just to get through the hour or the minute. As I got older, I realized depression is just a part of life, it just happens sometimes out of absolutely nowhere. Even now if I don't fill my days with activities I can still get down. It's never that you're cured but it's that you learn to manage or cope in healthier ways. I also learned sometimes it's ok to be bummed out. Some days you want and need to just lay around and feel bummed out, but you have to get up after that. One other exercise I practice is just spreading positivity. If I'm feeling down, I will go out of my way to just do little things whether its compliment the waitress in the restaurant or let someone in my lane while driving, just anything to be positive. Just throwing a smile at someone can be contagious and turn someone's day around. With technology we have kind of lost that human interaction. Everywhere you look bus benches, restaurants, airports, wherever there are total strangers in close proximity to one another buried in their phones. I do it too sometimes – oftentimes I am writing back students. Other times I am doing nothing at all. But I also will hear out the random person who approaches me and tells me their life story. It happens a lot. I don't know why. Maybe it's written on my face that I will listen. Truth is I will listen. As I see it, I owe it to people to listen because so many have listened to me over the years. We can learn a lot from each other just by sharing our stories and experiences.   That's how communication began in early times. People told stories and those stores were passed down from generation to generation. Everybody has a story. Everybody has their own life hack that they can share with another person. My story isn't necessarily extraordinary. I am just someone who shares it. Maybe that's the extraordinary part if anything, but I really don't want praise for that. This book is being way too nice to me. I am so happy that Randy threw some digs at me. I feel much more comfortable when people are poking fun at me than when they are complimenting me. I'm not looking for accolades. I'm just looking to contribute something positive to this world because I took a lot away. My purpose is to try every day to make good of the tragedy and pain that I caused. I will confess it feels good to help others. It is the best feeling that I know. It feels a billion times better than hurting others. I can tell you that. It feels amazing. It's my skateboarding, snowboarding, running, walking, skating, feeling, moving, breathing, living. It's everything. It's not the driving force behind what I do, but it sure is a sweet bonus and the only reward I really care to receive in return

I started speaking in schools eighteen years ago and I will continue to do so as long as the schools will have me. As long as anyone will have me. Any audience who can benefit from this story and its message. As long as it still makes a difference, I will be right here. I love doing this. I love speaking with and meeting everyone along the way while seeing new places. I love the feeling of rolling into a room I have never been and parking in front of crowd who are sizing me up, but because they are teenagers and because I am wearing Vans, black denim, a Ramones shirt and have tattoos they give me some leeway. I love watching the faces in the audience come along with me on the journey and seeing them laugh and cry and have moments of introspection along the way. I love it when an audience jumps to their feet at the end of a talk and gives me a thunderous standing ovation. Or when a principal warns me this is a rowdy crew you may have your hands full and then those rowdies are dialed in from my opening words welcoming me into their world and their lives because they know that I am one of them. Older yes, but a punk and young at heart always. I love it when I have barely finished a presentation and I grab my phone and see I have a message from an audience member who was moved or "really needed that." I love it when I am sitting on the couch at home with my cats Zeke and Carmelita just relaxing watching Netflix or whatever and my phone lights up and it's an Instagram message from a kid who is no longer a kid but they were a kid when they heard me speak and they just want to reach out and make sure I am ok and let me know that they are ok. They tell me that my story and message have stayed with them and that they are glad I am still doing this and that they hope I continue to keep doing this. You've all given me purpose and meaning to my life. The students are the reason I get out of bed every day. I thank you for giving me a platform. I thank you for giving me a purpose. I believe in you. I always will.

There's a long road ahead. So, if I don't quit... You don't quit.

10

Epilogue: Author's Perspective

"In writing this book I learned so much about my friend that I never knew. Dark times that friends don't always share and secrets never told. However, the hardest elements were the emotional live interviews ."

A friend invited me to a dinner party in the Hollywood Hills one late autumn night. He said it would be an eclectic group of friends, movie stars, musicians and well to do businessmen. I felt a little out of place, so I invited a buddy. As we ascended into the hills and found parking, we noticed a group of people walking into this beautiful house overlooking Sunset Blvd. Bottle of wine in hand we figured we had the right address. At least we hoped so. We walked in the open front door and looked around. The house was incredible. Easily a $4 million home with exquisite furnishings and everyone seemed so important. Only problem, I didn't see my friend who invited us anywhere. As I walked through a bit lost a guy approached me in a wheelchair. He looked at me and asked who I was there to see. I told him my friend's name and he responded "nah man, never heard of him, but you brought wine so that's cool we like gifts. You're welcome to stay, what's your name?" At this point, my friend turned the corner and welcomed me into the home. I looked back at the guy in the chair and he had the biggest grin on his face, just laughing. That's how I became friends with Kevin Brooks.

He can sense when you're feeling a bit awkward in a situation and he makes light of it. His attitude is completely earnest and disarming, even when he's picking on you as friends do, he does it in such a way that you never feel bullied or disrespected. He's a genuine person with a real heart of gold. As our friendship grew, I learned of his story. I didn't think too much of it, nor did I ever see the wheelchair anymore when we hung out. I felt, well, it's convenient I'll always have a place to sit. That's obviously a joke that Kevin would appreciate, and I would be remiss if I didn't throw one of those in this book.

I never understood what his story meant until I actually saw his presentation in Burbank, CA at their local high school. It's one thing to read the story in this book but it's completely another to see him in person and hear the words aloud from the man who lived them. I admit, I cried. From the back of an auditorium, with five hundred high schoolers in attendance I cried listening to my friend detail the horrific accident that bound him permanently to his chair. I think we all forget how privileged we are each day. The smallest things in life are taken for granted and sometimes I even catch myself. When I'm running late and I have to run up the stairs because the elevator is taking too long, or if I want to go for a hike with my wife and see Los Angeles from the top of a mountain. They seem like normal everyday occurrences and some days I tell her I can't be bothered with going. Imagine that, I can't be bothered. Meanwhile my friend will never be able to do these things again. I think as a fortunate soul we need to remember the simple things in life that are given to us and not take them for granted so easily. Even life itself. I'm not the first to admit I have battled depression throughout my life. And listening to the stories in this book as I did the interviews was not easy. The hardest being in speaking to Kevin's mother. I first did a 90-minute interview over the phone, she cried, I cried, and wouldn't you know it? The recording application on my phone didn't record more than 5 minutes of the entire 90. So, we did it again, and again. And each time the story is so heartbreaking, hearing from a mother's voice. The inflections and emotion. Each time I hung up that phone I called my own mother just to tell her "I love you". As you get older, you'll also see how important this is to do. You never realize how many lives you affect when you put yourself in danger, whether its drunk driving, suicidal thoughts or just reckless living with drugs and alcohol. But let me tell you, when you are on the other side and you listen to the stories firsthand of the people it affects, you will never think of those things as an option again. Just take it out of your head. Days that were, "not so great" for myself, I would call Kevin. I wouldn't let on to what was going on in my head, I would just talk to him. He has a way of immediately recognizing feeling and tone, whether he acknowledges it or not, but then he talks to you. And as people in the book have said, sometimes just talking to someone is all you need. To know you aren't alone, ever, is the single most important feeling.

And I can relate to a lot of the stories in this book. Whether it was struggling with drug addiction, suicidal tendencies or so often drinking and driving, I've been there. Plenty of nights I would drive home on Mulholland Dr in Los Angeles, down winding streets with no guard rails or streetlights. I would praise myself the next day for making it home and continue on to the same act next weekend never thinking anything bad would happen to me. I would listen to friends who would tell you, "its ok you're fine, here take this or have one more drink it's no big deal" and honestly, it was a big deal. I even have an iPhone video of myself swerving on a dark street at night, thinking my friends would be impressed that I made it home. Luckily, I did. But that could have gone so very wrong and I shouldn't be here looking back on the things I've done and someone else could be doing these interviews with my mother and asking her "how much she misses me".

These stupid things we do are all part of growing up. The feelings we have are real to us at the time. They may not be right though, and here I sit by the pool in 80-degree weather at my home on Sunset Blvd in Los Angeles, CA at 41 years old. I never thought I'd be here. My beautiful wife is out shopping while I sit here and relay this story. She doesn't even know the extent of things I've been through and maybe never will. But for those of you sitting there and reading this I want you to know. I know how you feel on those dark days. I know how you feel when you are cock sure and confident and think, one more drink I'll be fine. That was me in my infinite youthful invincibility. And I will be not the first or the last to tell you, you're wrong. At any given moment it can happen. Kevin is a visual and mental reminder of those consequences.

I've walked home from dinner with Kevin, he's fallen out of his chair when we hit a bump in the road and he'll yell at me, "pick me up, you jerk!" Even though we are both laughing it's in that moment that you realize your friend needs you. He can't walk home with you so easily as you normally do. And it's because of the decisions you make. I'm asking you please make the right decision, you all have so much to live for and if you're reading this at 17 and think 41 is old. I'll tell you it's not. You feel exactly the same way physically and mentally. And you have so many things that can happen in the blink of an eye for better or worse.

My whole life changed for the better one day, and then it got worse and better again and each time it gets better than before. But it's never over. Please remember that. You can overcome, no matter what the adversity. I watch my friend in a wheelchair still hold the most positive attitude and do things in life that I'm afraid of trying even with two able legs. If he can do it, then you can do it. You can do anything.

I only hope that in reading this book you find that message of hope. On days that are dark, and all seems to be lost just know it's one day, and you have a lifetime ahead of days that will be better. Also, in that one dark moment you may feel immediate relief, you will permanently hurt the ones you love forever. And it's not fair. Just make the right choices, you always have options. Know that its ok to say no. No one will think you're uncool or think less of you, honestly, they won't even think of you. Most people are too busy thinking about themselves. So, do the same. Think about you. Think about those close to you. Think about what really matters. Imagine a life ahead, full of dreams and ambition and know that you can get there. No one day can be as bad as missing a lifetime of greatness. I wish you all nothing but happiness and please take care of yourselves.

I'll leave you with two things that always helped me. Call me an old man, and as this book ages it'll seem older and older, but I like to listen to two different musicians for inspiration. The first is Eddie Vedder "I'm Still Here." And to paraphrase he says "So small, how could these struggles seem so big, so big. As the palms in the breeze still blow green and the waves still crash absolute blue. I'm still here. I imagine in a month or twelve I'll be laughing at a stupid joke and I'll see myself stopping short, and there I am all alone standing in grass and white headstones all in rows. I stop. Kneel. I picture a sober awakening a reawakening into the scene, sip my drink till the ice hits my lip and order another round." This quote has helped me many times. It helps in that you realize no problem is too big, time really does heal all wounds and there will be a day you feel better. On that day you'll look back at the life you have and the happy memories you've been afforded for doing the right thing. And you'll still here. Its ok to feel sad for a moment but know you made it through. You're stronger than you can ever imagine.

The last and most powerful to me was quoted by Stevie Ray Vaughan, arguably the greatest guitarist of all time who died in a helicopter crash at the age of thirty five years old. His song "Life Without You", he always stops mid solo to leave you with some knowledge and a message of positivity. Here is my favorite excerpt: "I'm glad to be with you today. You see it does me good to stop and think about this stuff because it's too easy to forget for a lot of us what we've been through where we've come from and where we are trying to get. Where we are trying to get is back home inside, and the love and caring that we have between us. See, it took me a long time to find out, but everything else is a bunch of something else. Cuz all I could do for a long time was run away from myself and everybody that cared you know. And usually that meant, run to the party and stay there for as long as possible. And then one day I nearly died, and it dawned on me that that was not the right thing to do. Cuz it is time to come home every once in a while. What this is all about is I'm asking you all to be there for the ones that need you and love you the most. And they need you all the time. I know I do." Prepare yourself. Cue the most goosebump inducing guitar solo you've ever experienced. Now, I heard these words for the first time almost twenty years ago. And to this day it helps.

As for Kevin, he keeps every single email anyone has ever written him and responds to everyone he can. So, for you, what that means is in those dark times or times of confusion just know someone out there does care. So please take care of yourselves for you and the ones that love you and know this. They do love you. Life isn't that hard its meant to be enjoyed and its much simpler than people make it. One very important point I do want to make though. Most people would resent or want to feel angry and blame Kevin for his stupid action that resulted in the death of his friend. However, what we need to remember is it could've been any one of us, he didn't commit this act with any malice or intended harm. It was an accident. An accident that irreparably changed two families forever. But, since this journey for him began he has spoken to countless teens struggling with addiction, depression and negative thoughts. And has made a real change. A friend lost his life that night, but in the last 17 years there are hundreds maybe even thousands of young men and women who will see tomorrow, who will spend the holidays with their families this year because of the positive message his presentations evoke. And he does this selflessly detailing his horrific past. And that is a good thing.

I can't imagine the incredibly heavy albatross Kevin wears each day nor can I imagine hearing the sad stories from kids day after day. But he does it. And he puts his own feelings aside for the betterment of others. We may tease one another as all friends do but I'm so fantastically proud of him, and even more so to call this person my friend. At the risk of overinflating his ego, I think Kevin misses how much good he actually does. The lives he touches, touches others. And those lives... others. People are alive today because of Kevin, those people are now called "Mom" by their children and they'll go on and grow and never knew that they may have not even had an opportunity at life. You've done a lot of good Kevin Brooks. And Kevin, you only have to do this as long as you want, but knowing you, you're going to do this until the figurative "wheels come off." And that's so great about you. You're an amazing man. Thank you for everything you do and who you are.

I also want to take a moment and thank everyone who participated in this book. Sharing your personal details and darkest moments must not have been easy, so I really want to thank each one of you for that and we can only hope it helps even one person in the future, and then it's all worth it. Love & Rock 'n Roll.

ABOUT THE AUTHORS

◆ ◆ ◆

Kevin Brooks is an inspirational speaker and comedian from Vancouver, British Columbia, Canada. In the past two decades he has spoken to hundreds of thousands of youths in schools, conferences and community events across North America. In his free time he enjoys hand cycling and cooking a strictly Vegan diet. He currently resides in Vancouver with his two cats, Carmelita and Zeke.

Jeff DeAngelis is an author and screenwriter currently living in Los Angeles, CA. In his free time he enjoys rock music, photography and getting punched in the face at the local boxing gym. He currently lives in West Hollywood, CA with his wife, Ashlee.

Made in the USA
Middletown, DE
29 January 2020

83855088R00083